Better Homes and Gardens®

# CHRISTMAS
## FROM THE HEART®

Volume 13

Meredith® Books
Des Moines, Iowa

**Better Homes and Gardens®**

# CHRISTMAS
## FROM THE HEART®

| | |
|---:|:---|
| **Editor:** | Carol Field Dahlstrom |
| **Writer and Project Designer:** | Susan M. Banker |
| **Graphic Designer:** | Catherine Brett |
| **Contributing Food Editor:** | Kristi Thomas |
| **Project Designers:** | Kristen Dietrich, Phyllis Dunstan, Allison May, Janet Petersma, Margaret Sindelar, Ann E. Smith, Jan Temeyer, Alice Wetzel |
| **Technical Assistant:** | Judy Bailey |
| **Copy Chief:** | Terri Fredrickson |
| **Publishing Operations Manager:** | Karen Schirm |
| **Managers, Book Production:** | Pam Kvitne, Marjorie J. Schenkelberg, Rick von Holdt, Mark Weaver |
| **Contributing Copy Editor:** | Margaret Smith |
| **Contributing Proofreaders:** | Karen Grossman, Jessica Kearney Heidgerken, Susan J. Kling |
| **Photographers:** | Peter Krumhardt, Scott Little, Andy Lyons Cameraworks |
| **Photostyling Assistant:** | Donna Chesnut |
| **Technical Illustrator:** | Shawn Drafahl, Chris Neubauer Graphics, Inc. |
| **Editorial Assistants:** | Kaye Chabot, Cheryl Eckert, Karen McFadden |
| **Edit and Design Production Coordinator:** | Mary Lee Gavin |

### MEREDITH® BOOKS

| | |
|---:|:---|
| **Editor in Chief:** | Linda Raglan Cunningham |
| **Design Director:** | Matt Strelecki |
| **Executive Editor:** | Jennifer Dorland Darling |
| **Managing Editor:** | Gregory H. Kayko |

| | |
|---:|:---|
| **Publisher:** | James D. Blume |
| **Executive Director, Marketing:** | Jeffrey Myers |
| **Executive Director, New Business Development:** | Todd M. Davis |
| **Executive Director, Sales:** | Ken Zagor |
| **Director, Operations:** | George A. Susral |
| **Director, Production:** | Douglas M. Johnston |
| **Business Director:** | Jim Leonard |

| | |
|---:|:---|
| **Vice President and General Manager:** | Douglas J. Guendel |

### BETTER HOMES AND GARDENS® MAGAZINE

| | |
|---:|:---|
| **Editor in Chief:** | Karol DeWulf Nickell |

### MEREDITH PUBLISHING GROUP

| | |
|---:|:---|
| **President, Publishing Group:** | Stephen M. Lacy |
| **Vice President-Publishing Director:** | Bob Mate |

### MEREDITH CORPORATION

| | |
|---:|:---|
| **Chairman and Chief Executive Officer:** | William T. Kerr |

# Better Homes and Gardens®
# CHRISTMAS
## FROM THE HEART®

# contents

# glorious trees and trims

*Create a glowing Christmas tree as the focal point of your holiday decorating.*

SET A FESTIVE MOOD with a holiday tree decked with the colors and symbols of the season. **Tooled Stars,** *above* and *opposite*, have layered metals and interesting texture. Add gold silk to the mix with **Tufted Button Stars,** *above* and *opposite*, to make a heavenly statement. **Fluffy-Cuff Mittens,** *opposite*, lend a touch of red. Instructions are on pages 18–19.

Even when time runs short, you can make several of the ornaments shown on these two pages. Start with **Frosted Ornaments** to add sparkle to the tree. Shown, *above left*, in gold and red adorned with silver, you can use any color to coordinate with your holiday decorating scheme. As regal as kings' crowns, the **Jeweled Ornaments,** *above right*, bring elegance to a tree with a trio of frosted jewel tones. Make simple **Zigzagged Trims,** *opposite*, to hang on the tree or as the focal point of a holiday centerpiece. The instructions for the ornaments begin on page 19.

For a nontraditional holiday color palette, **Whimsy Hearts,** *opposite,* and **Tissued Treasures,** *above,* are purely delightful. The lightweight hearts are created from clay to hang gracefully from even the daintiest branches. The tissued balls are so easy to make that the kids can get in on the fun. Instructions to make these colorful trims are on pages 20–21.

If you want an old-world theme for your tree, then you'll love these quick and easy ideas. The **Merry Medallions,** *above* and *opposite*, are created from decorative pressed wood available in home centers. They are coated with color and gilded for shine. **Fancy Finials** and **Wondrous Wheels,** *opposite*, are wood pieces dressed up quickly with paint, gems, and ribbon. Resplendent in red and gold, these ornaments give a warm glow to the centerpiece of your holiday home. Instructions are on page 21.

Colored glass adds shimmer to your evergreen branches. **Rainbow Glass** ornaments, *left*, are one-of-a-kind decorations that are fun to create. Paint is applied inside each ornament, so the finished product is a surprise. **Wild Wire Hearts,** *above*, make a playful statement on a holiday package or tree. With the variety of beads available, each heart can be entirely different. Instructions are on page 22.

Encircle your Christmas tree with a **Wintry Garland** of white snowflakes strung on a red satin ribbon, *above*. For a personal touch, create **Picture-Perfect Ornaments,** *below*, for each member of the family. Let naturally bright red **Cranberry Creations**, *opposite*, add dimension and texture to a mix of trims. Instructions are on pages 22–23.

**Tooled Stars**

**Fluffy-Cuff Mittens**

## Tooled Stars

*shown on pages 6–7, and 9*

### WHAT YOU NEED

Paper; pencil; scissors
1 sheet each of light brass,
    aluminum, and copper, such
    as ArtEmboss
Texture stencils, such as American
    Traditional Stencils
Embossing tool; double-sided tape
⅛-inch hole punch; wood skewer
20-gauge wire in brass, steel, and
    copper
Clear silver-lined seed beads
Round-nose pliers

### HERE'S HOW

**1** Enlarge and trace the patterns, *below*, and cut out. Roll out each sheet of metal. Trace one large star and one small star on contrasting sheets of metal. Cut out all six stars.
**2** For each small star, lay the desired texture stencil on the star. Emboss the pattern onto the metal using the embossing tool.
**3** For each large star, lay the desired texture stencil on the star. Emboss the pattern on the edges or the entire star.
**4** Affix the small stars to the large stars using double-sided tape. Punch a hole in the top of each ornament.
**5** Wrap 12 inches of brass, steel, and copper wire around skewer to coil. Twist the ends to secure and thread wire ends through a hole. Thread one seed bead on each twisted wire. Coil remaining wire ends with round-nose pliers.

## Fluffy-Cuff Mittens

*shown on page 7*

### WHAT YOU NEED

Lamb's Pride (85% wool/15%
    mohair) worsted-weight
    single-ply yarn (4 ounce skein;
    approximately 190 yards) in
    M80-I or M64-1
Scissors
50-gram ball of Stars (50%
    viscosa/50%poliammide)
    polyamid-nylon eyelash yarn
Size 3 and 5 double-pointed
    knitting needles (dpns)
Ruler; yarn needle
2 stitch holders; stitch marker
Tracing paper; pencil
3-inch square of white wool felt
Fabric glue or needle and thread
Snowflake charm
Yarn needle

**GAUGE:** Knitting every rnd for
    stockinette stitch (St st) and
    with larger dpns, 5 sts and
    5 rnds = 1 inch

### ABBREVIATIONS:

dpn(s) = double-pointed needle(s)
k = knit
p = purl
rnd(s) = round(s)
st(s) = stitch(es)
St st = stockinette stitch
tog = together

**Tooled Stars Patterns**
**reproduce at 300%**

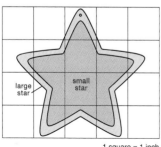

large
star

small
star

1 square = 1 inch

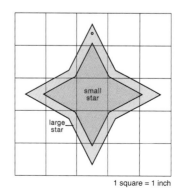

large
star

small
star

1 square = 1 inch

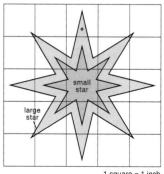

large
star

small
star

1 square = 1 inch

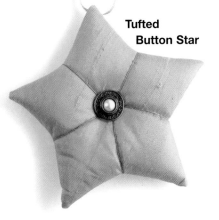

**Tufted Button Star**

## HERE'S HOW

**1** With smaller dpns and one strand of each yarn held together, cast on 28 sts. Arrange the sts onto 3 dpns; join and place a marker to indicate the beginning of rnd. Work around in k1, p1 ribbing for 2 inches.

**2** Change to larger dpns. Knit every rnd for St st until the mitten measures 2¾ inches from beginning.

**3** For thumb, slip 6 sts onto holder; cast on 6 sts, k around = 28 sts. Work even to 4¾ inches from beginning.

**4** For shaping, Rnd 1: (K2, k2 tog) around. Rnd 2: K21 sts. Rnd 3: (K1, k2 tog) around. Rnd 4: K14 sts. Rnd 5: (K2 tog) around = 7 sts.

**5** Cut yarn leaving 8-inch tail. Thread tail into needle and back through remaining sts. Pull up to gather; close top opening. Secure.

**6** To complete thumb, join yarn and k6 sts from holder, pick up and k6 more sts around opening. Arrange the 12 sts onto 3 dpn; join. Work around in St st until thumb measures 1¼ inches from beginning. K2 tog around. Leaving a 6-inch tail, cut yarn. Thread tail into yarn needle and back through remaining sts. Close opening; secure in place.

**7** Block the mitten to shape with thumb to side. Trace the star pattern, *below*, onto tracing paper; cut out. Use pattern to cut a star from felt. Use fabric glue or hand-stitch felt star and snowflake charm to mitten. Use a short length of yarn for the hanger.

## Tufted Button Stars

*shown on pages 6–7*

### WHAT YOU NEED

Tracing paper; pencil
Scissors
¼ yard gold douppioni silk
¼ yard lightweight fusible
    interfacing
Needle and thread
Cotton batting; shank button
Gold lamé embroidery thread
½ yard of ¼-inch-wide gold ribbon

### HERE'S HOW

**1** Enlarge and trace the star pattern, *below*, onto tracing paper. Cut out the shape. (The pattern includes a ¼-inch seam allowance.) Use the pattern to cut two stars from silk. Make a slit on the star back. Line silk pieces with fusible interfacing and trim at silk edges.

**2** Right sides facing, use tiny stitches to stitch the front to the back. To reinforce stitching at the inside angles of the star, stitch a second time. Trim and clip seams. Turn to the right side through the back slit.

**3** Add batting to shape the star. Stitch the opening closed.

**4** With gold lamé thread, tuft star around the inside angles and through the center. Sew a button to the center. Attach a loop of gold ribbon to a point for hanging.

**Frosted Ornaments**

## Frosted Ornaments

*shown on page 8*

### WHAT YOU NEED

Crystal clear micro beads
Plastic cup
3-D fabric paint in silver glitter,
    such as Scribbles
Ornament with a smooth
    satin finish; shallow container

### HERE'S HOW

**1** Pour micro beads in cup. Set aside.

**2** Apply paint on the top of the ornament to create a drizzled snowcap effect. Hold ornament over empty container and gently pour micro beads over the painted area. Hang ornament to dry at least 24 hours. Pour leftover beads back into the cup.

**3** Apply paint on the bottom of the ornament. Hold the ornament over the container and gently pour the tiny beads over the wet paint. Hang ornament to dry at least 24 hours.

## Fluffy-Cuff Mitten—
## Full-Size Star Pattern

## Tufted Button Star—Pattern
## reproduce at 400%

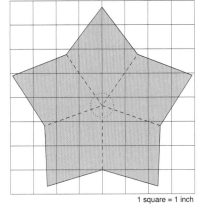

1 square = 1 inch

**Zigzagged Trims**

## Zigzagged Trims

shown on page 9

### WHAT YOU NEED

Shiny red ball ornaments
3-D fabric paint in glittering gold,
such as Scribbles
Gold iridescent glaze
Paintbrush

### HERE'S HOW

**1** Using gold paint, squiggle six lines on one side of each ornament. Let dry. Squiggle six additional lines on the opposite side. Let dry.
**2** Brush three coats of iridescent glaze on every other section of the ornaments, allowing to dry after each coat.

## Jeweled Ornaments

shown on page 8

### WHAT YOU NEED

2½-inch jewel-color ornaments
⅝-inch gold metallic ribbon
Ruler
Scissors
Acrylic jewel rhinestones to
fit ribbon
Black marker
Waxed paper
Tape
3-D fabric glitter paint in gold
¼-inch double-sided tape
Crafts glue, such as Goop

### HERE'S HOW

**1** Remove the ornament cap. For each ornament, cut two 10-inch lengths of gold ribbon. Tuck one end of one length of ribbon into ornament opening.
**2** Space rhinestones on ribbon. Mark the center of each rhinestone on the ribbon. Remove ribbon from ornament and lay both ribbons flat on waxed paper; tape in place. Mark the second ribbon with the rhinestone spacing.
**3** Glue rhinestones on the ribbons using gold glitter paint. Outline each rhinestone with glitter paint. Let dry at least 24 hours.
**4** Apply double-sided tape to the back of the ribbon. Apply double-sided tape to the outer neck of the ornament. Tuck one end of one length of ribbon into ornament. Press ribbon against taped neck and wrap ribbon around ornament. Repeat process with second ribbon, placing it perpendicular to the first ribbon.
**5** Slightly spread the prongs on the ornament cap. Apply glue to the inside of cap. Place on the ornament and gently squeeze to secure over ribbons. Let the glue dry.

**Whimsy Hearts**

## Whimsy Hearts

shown on page 10

### WHAT YOU NEED

White air-dry clay, such as Crayola
Model Magic
Rolling pin
Heart-shape cookie cutters
Retractable pen
Decorative scissors
Scissors
Toothpick
Acrylic paints in lime green, hot
pink, and orange
Paintbrush
Yarn

### HERE'S HOW

**1** On a protected work surface, use a rolling pin to flatten clay between ⅛ to ¼ inches. Cut out shapes with cookie cutters. If desired, cut out small hearts from the centers of large hearts.
**2** Create dotted texture by using a retractable pen with cartridge retracted and pressing gently into surface.
**3** Cut strips of rolled clay using decorative scissors. Lay the strips on hearts in a pattern.
**4** Cut out clay holly leaves with scissors. Roll small clay balls. Press balls and leaves into surface.
**5** Make holes for hanging with a toothpick. Let the clay dry.
**6** Paint the ornament sections different colors. Let the paint dry.
**7** Thread yarn through holes to make a loop for hanging. Knot ends together.

**Jeweled
Ornaments**

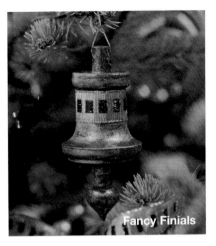

**Tissued Treasures**

**Fancy Finials**

**3** Screw an eye hook in the top of the wheel. Glue a gem in the wheel center on each side. Let the glue dry.
**4** Thread gold cord through the eye hook; knot the cord ends.

## Merry Medallions

*shown on pages 12–13*

**WHAT YOU NEED**

Ornate wood appliqués
Drill and 3/16-inch bit
Fine sandpaper
Wood sealer
Paintbrush
Acrylic paints in red and
   metallic gold
Paint sponge
Bowl of water
Paper towels

**HERE'S HOW**

**1** For each ornament, carefully drill a hole for hanging. Sand the rough wood around the drilled hole.
**2** Place the ornament on newspaper and prime with wood sealer. Let the sealer dry. Lightly sand the raised wood grain.
**3** Paint the ornament red or gold. Let dry. Apply a second coat and let dry.
**4** Sponge or brush one coat of gold paint on a red ornament. Immediately wipe it off with a water-dampened paper towel. Add more gold paint using a fine brush in the recesses of the appliqué to accent the design. Let dry. Use the same process to add red paint in the recesses of the gold-painted ornaments. Let dry.

## Tissued Treasures

*shown on page 11*

**WHAT YOU NEED**

Scissors
Tissue paper in assorted colors
Thick white crafts glue
Water
Small dish
Large round clear glass ornament
Paintbrush
Glitter in desired color

**HERE'S HOW**

**1** Use scissors to cut tissue paper into small squares.
**2** Mix a solution of 1 tablespoon water and 1 tablespoon glue in a small dish. Brush a small section of the ornament with the mixture. Use the damp paintbrush to pick up a square of tissue paper and place it on the wet section of the ornament. Brush a coat of the mixture on the paper. Add paper squares, randomly overlapping and angling papers or making a pattern to cover the ornament.
**3** After ball is covered with paper squares, brush on a final coat of the glue and water mixture. If desired, dust with glitter. Let dry.

## Fancy Finials

*shown on page 13*

**WHAT YOU NEED**

Wood finial ornament
Acrylic paints in red and
   metallic gold
Paintbrush
Scissors
Red and gold metallic ribbon
Thick white crafts glue
Metallic gold cord

**HERE'S HOW**

**1** Paint the ornament red. Let dry.
**2** Dab a small amount of gold paint on the brush and dust the ornament with gold, allowing the red to show through. Let the paint dry.
**3** Cut ribbon to wrap around ornament. Glue in place. Let dry.
**4** Thread the gold cord through the ornament; knot the cord ends.

## Wondrous Wheels

*shown on page 13*

**WHAT YOU NEED**

Wood wheels
Acrylic paints in red and
   metallic gold
Paintbrush
Screw eye hook
Round acrylic gems
Thick white crafts glue
Metallic gold cord; scissors

**HERE'S HOW**

**1** Paint the wheel red. Let dry.
**2** Dab a small amount of gold paint on the brush and dust the ornament with gold, allowing the red to show through. Let the paint dry.

**Wondrous Wheels**

**Merry Medallions**

## Rainbow Glass

*shown on pages 14–15*

### WHAT YOU NEED

Clear glass ornaments
Rubbing alcohol; paper towels
Glass paints, such as Pēbēo Vitrea,
    in assorted colors; scissors
Paintbrush; 20-gauge copper wire

### HERE'S HOW

**1** Swirl a small amount of rubbing alcohol inside the ornament; rinse with water. Let dry.

**2** Paint one ornament at a time, using a brush to drop small amounts of paint into the ornament. Begin with one color and add the next color while the previous color is still wet.

**3** Cut 2-inch lengths of copper wire and shape into S hooks to hang the ornaments to dry. Bake the ornaments in the oven according to the glass paint manufacturer's directions. Let cool.

## Wild Wire Hearts

*shown on page 15*

### WHAT YOU NEED

Armature modeling wire
Protective eyewear
Wire cutters
20-gauge steel wire or
    22-gauge black wire
Assorted glass beads
Needle-nose pliers

### HERE'S HOW

**1** Bend armature wire into a heart shape, forming a loop with the wire ends.

**2** Wear protective eyewear and cut one long piece of steel or black wire approximately 3 feet long.

**3** Wrap wire around the heart and bead as desired. Use needle-nose pliers to tighten the wire ends around the armature wire.

Rainbow Glass

## Wintry Garland

*shown on page 16*

.

### WHAT YOU NEED

¼-inch-wide red satin ribbon
¾-inch red plastic star beads
2- to 2½-inch foam snowflakes,
    available in crafts stores
Tapestry needle

### HERE'S HOW

**1** To make a 1-yard-long garland, use 1½ yards of ribbon, and alternate six snowflakes with seven star beads. Tie a star bead at one end of the ribbon.

**2** Thread ribbon in and out through the snowflake cutouts, wrapping a section to secure. Leave 6 inches between items.

Wild Wire Hearts

Wintry Garland

## Cranberry Creations

*shown on page 17*

### WHAT YOU NEED

3-inch-diameter plastic-foam ball
Red acrylic paint
Paintbrush
6-inch length of ½-inch-wide
 red ribbon
Hot-glue gun and glue sticks
Artificial cranberries

### HERE'S HOW

**1** Paint the plastic foam ball red. Let the paint dry.
**2** Fold the ribbon in half to make a loop; hot-glue the ends to the foam ball.
**3** Hot-glue the berries to the foam ball to cover the entire surface.

## Picture-Perfect Ornaments

*shown on page 16*

### WHAT YOU NEED

Pencil
Ruler
Sheet of birch craft wood
Newspaper

Picture Perfect Ornaments

Crafts knife
2 square photo frames, such as
 Card Connection
Metallic gold spray paint, such as
 Krylon 18kt Gold
2½ yards of red ribbon
Permanent adhesive, such as
 Gem-Tac
¼-inch double-sided tape
Bugle beads in several colors
Gold micro beads
Scissors
Shallow container
Photograph

### HERE'S HOW

**1** Measure and mark two 4½-inch squares on craft wood. On a protected work surface, cut the wood using a crafts knife and ruler as a guide. Lay frames on each wood square. Center and mark an internal square on the wood inside the frame. Cut out the square.
**2** In a well-ventilated work area, spray the wood with two coats of gold paint, allowing drying time between coats.

**3** Cut two 24-inch lengths of ribbon. Wrap each one through a square opening, centering ribbon at top of opening. Using permanent adhesive, glue ribbon in place on both sides. Cut two 7-inch lengths of ribbon to wrap the lower portions of the frames; glue in place. Cut two 11-inch lengths of ribbon. Loop each ribbon and glue to back of ornament for a hanger. Glue a frame to front of each ornament in square opening. If needed, lay a heavy book over frame to secure in place. Let the glue dry.
**4** Apply double-sided tape to wood around the outer edges of frames. Sprinkle bugle beads on taped areas over a shallow container. Shake off excess beads and remove beads from container. Sprinkle micro beads onto taped areas to fill in any gaps. Shake off excess beads.
**5** Tie the ribbons at top of ornament frames into bows. Tape a photograph to the back of each ornament to show through the openings.

Cranberry Creations

# candles all aglow

*Flickering candlelight from pretty candles creates a warm welcome.*

CANDLES BECOME EXTRAORDINARY when you add a few creative touches. **Joyfully Sealed Candles,** *above,* are regal with metallic gold seals on purple. **Berry Brights,** *opposite,* sparkle with a colorful mix of miniature beads cascading around the edges. Instructions are on page 36.

*Glistening glass beads and easy-bend copper wire*

Shape an unexpected centerpiece with **Contemporary Copper,** *opposite*. Embellish copper-color candles with beaded wires in holiday designs. For votives, decorate a mesh holder like the

## add instant appeal to candles and their holders.

one, *above*, with beaded wire spirals for a **Dripping in Gold** effect. Use transparent beads for both of these candle arrangements, as they will beautifully reflect the flickering candlelight. Instructions are on page 37.

**Eucalyptus Lights,** *above,* are ringed in fragrant greenery and baubles for a freshly jeweled combination. Styled after dangling earrings, **Beaded Votives,** *opposite,* combine hardware store finds with beaded fringes. This technique transforms the simplest glass holders into festive table decorations. Instructions are on page 38.

Embellish cone-shape candles with tooled designs for **Carved Christmas Pillars,** *opposite*. Highlight the designs with metallic gold paint. For miniature elegance, cut ornate shapes from metal, trim with gems, and tool the edges to make **Royal Collars,** *above*. Instructions are on page 39.

Replace the candle as needed, but keep the **Beaded Candle Plate,** *above*, to bring sparkle to the table every holiday season. Combine metal with colorful beads to embellish pillar candles that are **Fit for a King,** *opposite*. Wrapping the candle or pinned to one side, these classy creations are works of art. Instructions are on page 40.

Embed tiny decorative tiles in candle surfaces to make **Mosaic Tile Candles**, *opposite*. Frame the miniature tiles with beads and sequins at each point. Radiant **Stained-Glass Pillars**, *above*, pay tribute to stained-glass windows. Candle-painting medium makes the magical images adhere. Full instructions are on page 41.

Joyfully Sealed Candles

## Joyfully Sealed Candles

*shown on page 24*

**WHAT YOU NEED**
  Purple pillar candles
  Paper towels
  Rubbing alcohol
  20-gauge gold wire and
     needle-nose pliers, optional
  Waxed paper
  Rubber stamp stick
  Gold ink pad
  Matches
  Gold sealing wax

**HERE'S HOW**
**1** Wipe the candle surface with a paper towel and rubbing alcohol. Let dry.
**2** If desired, wrap gold wire around a pillar candle and twist the ends to secure.
**3** Cover work surface with waxed paper. Stamp rubber stamp in gold ink pad. Light a stick of gold sealing wax; drip hot wax in a circle on the waxed paper. Immediately insert rubber stamp in hot wax and let the stamp remain until wax has cooled. Gently peel the seal from the waxed paper.

**4** To affix seals to pillar candles, light the stick of gold sealing wax and put a drop of hot wax onto the candle surface. Immediately apply the wax seal to the candle, gently pressing. Let cool.

## Berry Brights

*shown on page 25*

**WHAT YOU NEED**
  Red pillar candles
  Paper towels
  Rubbing alcohol
  Assorted red and gold micro
     beads, such as Micro Mosaics
  Paper cup
  Candle-painting medium
  Small paintbrush; shallow container

**HERE'S HOW**
**1** Wipe candle surface with a paper towel and rubbing alcohol. Let dry.
**2** Pour beads into a cup. Using a paintbrush, apply candle paint medium to candle, creating snowcap effect. Hold the pillar candle over the shallow container. Gently pour the micro beads on the painted areas. Let the candle paint medium dry for several hours.

Berry Brights

Contemporary Copper

Dripping In Gold

## Contemporary Copper

*shown on page 26*

### WHAT YOU NEED

Tracing paper; pencil
20-gauge copper wire; wire snips
Needle-nose pliers
Amber-color small round beads in round and teardrop shapes
24-gauge gold wire
Crafts glue, such as Goop
Copper-color pillar candles

### HERE'S HOW

**1** Enlarge and trace the desired shape pattern, *below.*

**2** *For the crown-shape beaded wire,* bend copper wire using the pattern as a guide. Snip off excess. Thread a small amber bead through a 3-inch length of gold wire. Bend both wire ends and thread through an amber teardrop bead. Wire the ends to the top until all five free-form points are wired with beads. Gently insert ½ inch of wire ends into candle.

**3** *For the beaded spirals,* cut four 8-inch lengths of copper wire. Shape each wire into a coil, using the pattern as a guide. Thread five or six small amber beads and one teardrop bead on each coiled wire. Glue in place. Let dry. Use needle-nose pliers to straighten the lower ½ inch on each wire end. Gently push straightened wire ends into candle.

**4** *For the beaded tree,* cut five 18-inch lengths of copper wire. Shape each wire into a tree, using the pattern as a guide to bend the wire back and forth. Thread one small bead on wire at top of tree. Glue in place. Thread three small amber beads at the tree base. Gently insert ½ inch of wire end into pillar candle.

## Dripping in Gold

*shown on page 27*

### WHAT YOU NEED

Copper mesh, such as American Art Clay Co.
Ruler; square glass vase
Wire snips; scissors; glass beads
Gold wire in 20- and 24-gauge size
Round-nose pliers; wood skewer
Newspapers; votive candle

### HERE'S HOW

**1** Fold a hem in the bottom of mesh using the edge of a ruler. Bend a vertical hem on one side of the mesh. Wrap mesh around vase and trim excess for a small overlap along one corner.

**2** Coil 20-gauge wire around a wood skewer. Cut wire as desired and thread beads on one end of each wire. Bend a loop at one end of wire using round-nose pliers. Attach beaded coils to mesh front, back, and sides.

**3** Tightly wrap mesh around glass container and secure the mesh together with four 3-inch lengths of 24-gauge wire. Thread the wires through the mesh at all four points before you twist the wire tightly at each point. Twist the wires to secure. Place a votive candle in the holder.

*Note:* Never leave a burning candle unattended or in reach of children.

### Contemporary Copper—Spiral, Crown, and Tree Patterns

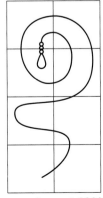

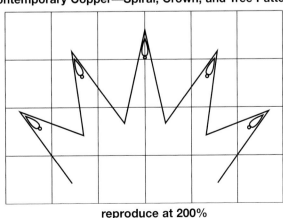

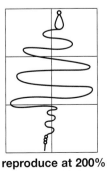

**reproduce at 200%**
1 square = 1 inch

**reproduce at 200%**
1 square = 1 inch

**reproduce at 200%**
1 square = 1 inch

## Eucalyptus Lights

*shown on page 28*

**WHAT YOU NEED**

Pillar candles
Real or artificial eucalyptus stems
2-inch eye pins
Gold bell caps
Gold bead cones
Gold silver-lined seed beads
Wire snips
Round-nose pliers
6mm jump rings
28-gauge brass wire
Needle-nose pliers
Ruler

**HERE'S HOW**

**1** Wrap the eucalyptus stems around candles. Leaving a small overlap, snip off excess. Remove stems.

**2** Thread eye pins with a bead cone, bell cap, and gold bead. Snip off excess wire, leaving ¼ inch to bend into a loop using round-nose pliers. Attach beaded eye pins to each eucalyptus stem between leaves using a jump ring and needle-nose pliers.

**3** Cut 4-inch lengths of brass wire. Wrap eucalyptus stems around candles. Wrap the ends of the eucalyptus stems together with wire to secure. Tighten the wire with needle-nose pliers.

**4** Add one beaded eye pin to cover the wired stem.

**Eucalyptus Lights**

## Beaded Votives

*shown on page 29*

**WHAT YOU NEED**

Hose clamps, approximately
   3 inches in diameter, available at
   hardware stores
Glass votive candleholders
Wire snips
24-gauge gold wire; newspapers
Sandable primer for metal
Gold spray paint, such as Krylon
   18kt gold
5mm jewelry bells

2-inch gold eye pins
Assorted glass and metal beads
Round-nose pliers
Gold jewelry chain
6mm gold jump rings
Needle-nose pliers

**HERE'S HOW**

**1** Snip off closures on each hose clamp. Bend the hose band ends together to form a ring to slip inside the candleholder. Wire the band closed with gold wire.

**2** In a well-ventilated work area, cover the work surface with newspapers. Spray each band with primer. Let dry. Spray the band with gold paint. Let dry.

**3** Attach jewelry bells to eye pins using needle-nose pliers. Thread assorted beads on eye pin. Snip off excess, leaving ¼ inch at top of wire to bend into a loop using round-nose pliers. Attach a ¼-inch jewelry chain to each beaded eye pin loop. Attach a jump ring to the opposite end of the jewelry chain; attach the jump ring to the band using needle-nose pliers.

**Beaded Votives**

Carved Christmas Pillars

Royal Collars

10mm faceted square rhinestones
Gem glue, such as Glass, Metal &
    More Embossing tool
2¼-inch candle in glass holder

**HERE'S HOW**
**1** Trace or photocopy the candle collar pattern, *below*. Lay out sheet of brass on a soft surface such as foam or cardboard. Tape pattern to brass.
**2** Using the embossing tool, trace over the pattern.
**3** Cut out the outside edges of candle collar. Using the tip of a scissors, puncture a hole in the center of the collar. Cut the interior lines of the collar. Bend the cut triangles downward through the collar. Coil each piece up using round-nose pliers.
**4** Glue rhinestones to brass candle collar. Let the glue dry. Set the collar on the candleholder.

## Carved Christmas Pillars
*shown on page 30*

**WHAT YOU NEED**
    Paper towels
    Pickle fork
    Crafts knife
    Red cone-shape candles
    Acrylic paints in metallic gold and
        cardinal red
    Candle- and soap-painting
        medium, such as Delta
    Small paintbrush

**HERE'S HOW**
**1** Spread paper towels on a work surface. Make fork carvings on a candle, dragging the pickle fork in short or long strokes, or keep the fork in one spot while twisting the candle to create a circle or half circle. Remove excess wax and smooth carved surfaces with a crafts knife.
**2** Mix gold paint with candle-painting medium. Highlight carved areas with gold paint using your finger or a brush. Wipe off excess with a paper towel. Let dry.
**3** Mix red paint with candle-painting medium. Highlight candle surface with red paint using your finger or a brush. Wipe off excess with a paper towel. Let dry.

## Royal Collars
*shown on page 31*

**WHAT YOU NEED**
    Tracing paper and pencil or
        photocopier
    Lightweight brass sheet, such as
        ArtEmboss; tape
    Foam or cardboard
    Embossing tool
    Scissors
    Round-nose
        pliers

**Royal Collars Pattern**

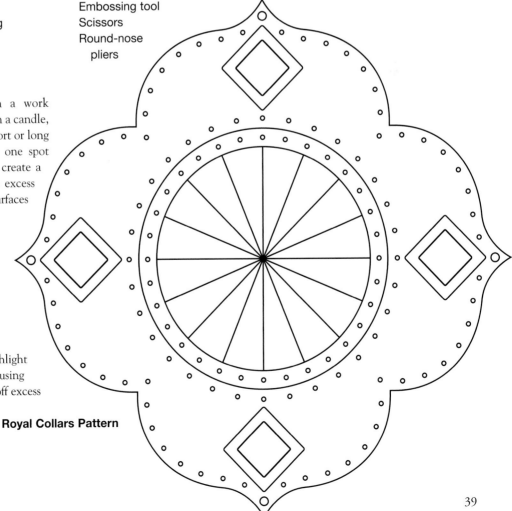

39

Beaded Candle Plate

## Beaded Candle Plate

*shown on page 32*

### WHAT YOU NEED

    Frosted candle plates
    Pillar candles
    Permanent adhesive, such as
      Gem-Tac
    Metallic green, blue, and purple
      silver-lined seed beads
    Paper cups
    Shallow container
    Gold micro beads

### HERE'S HOW

**1** Wash and dry a candle plate. Place a pillar candle on a candle plate. Apply adhesive directly to candle plate all the way around the pillar candle. Remove the candle.

**2** Pour metallic beads into a paper cup. Lay the candle plate in a shallow container. Gently shake the beads on the plate. Gently pour off excess beads. Pour beads back into cup. Pour tiny beads into a paper cup. Gently shake the beads on the plate to fill in between larger beads. Gently pour off the excess micro beads. Let the plate dry 24 hours before using.

Fit for a King Candles

## Fit for a King

*shown on page 33*

### WHAT YOU NEED

    Lightweight aluminum metal, such
      as Art Emboss
    Ruler
    Scissors
    Templates, such as American
      Traditional Stencils, in braided
      borders, triple border, and
      Mediterranean tile motifs
    Embossing tool or pen
    Paper towels
    Antique gold buffing medium, such
      as Rub 'n Buff
    Pillar candles
    Gold fleck beads
    Wire snips
    Round glass gold beads
    8mm gold hologram sequins
    Straight pins
    ⅛-inch hole punch
    2-inch head pins
    Round-nose pliers
    6mm jump rings
    Needle-nose pliers

### HERE'S HOW

**1** For the tall pillar collar, roll out the aluminum. Measure and cut a 3×12-inch strip. Lay braided borders template on aluminum and trace designs with embossing tool or pen. This will be the back side of the metal.

**2** Turn embossed metal strip face up on a paper towel. Using your finger, apply buffing medium to front of tooled metal following the manufacturer's directions. Let dry.

**3** Wrap embossed metal strip around candle. Allow to overlap ½ inch and cut off excess. Shorten straight pins to ½ inch by snipping with wire snips. Secure strip to candle using two straight pins and two glass gold beads. Decorate seam of strip with three sets of straight pins, glass gold beads, gold fleck beads, and gold sequins. Continue this pattern twice around the candle.

**4** For the medium pillar collar, roll out aluminum. Measure and cut a 2½-inch square. Lay Mediterranean tile template on aluminum and trace design with embossing tool or pen. This will be the back side of the metal.

**5** Turn embossed metal square faceup on a paper towel. Using finger, apply buffing medium to front of tooled metal following the manufacturer's directions. Let dry.

**6** Lay embossed metal on candle. Shorten straight pins to ½ inch by snipping excess with wire snips. Secure the four corners with straight pins, glass gold beads, gold fleck beads, and gold sequins. Decorate the edges of the square with straight pins, glass gold beads, and gold fleck beads.

**7** For the short pillar collar, roll out the aluminum. Measure and cut a 2×12-inch strip. Lay triple border template on aluminum and trace design with embossing tool or pen. This will be the back side of the metal. Cut a triangle edge along the bottom of the strip. Punch holes on every other point using a ⅛-inch hole punch.

**8** Turn embossed metal strip faceup on a paper towel. Using finger, apply buffing medium to front of tooled metal following the manufacturer's directions. Let dry.

**9** Thread head pin with glass gold bead, gold fleck bead, gold sequin, and two additional glass gold beads. Snip off excess wire, leaving ¼ inch to bend into a loop using round-nose pliers. Attach the beaded head pins to the triangles of embossed metal strip using jump rings and needle-nose pliers.

**10** Wrap embossed metal strip around candle. Allow an overlap of ½ inch and cut off excess. Secure strip to candle using three straight pins and three glass gold beads.

## Mosaic Tile Candles

*shown on page 34*

### WHAT YOU NEED

Small mosaic glass tiles, such as Distinctive Details, in green and red; square candles
Crafts knife; wood cuticle tool
Rubbing alcohol; paper towels
Assorted black glass beads
8mm metallic gold hologram flat sequins
1-inch metallic gold head pins
Wire snips

### HERE'S HOW

**1** Lay a mosaic tile on a candle and score the outline of tile into the candle surface using a crafts knife. Remove the tile and carefully remove the candle wax within the outline so the tile can set flush with the candle surface.

**2** Lay the tile back on the candle. Use the wood cuticle tool's pointed edge to further score the tile outline. Use the cuticle pusher edge to scrape the layers of candle wax out. Continue this process until the tiles are embedded in the wax. Remove excess wax from the tile surface with rubbing alcohol and paper towels.

**3** Thread black beads and gold sequins on head pins to highlight the four corners of each tile. Using wire snips, cut the head pins off leaving approximately ¼ inch of wire. Insert into candles. Insert head pins in between the four corners on each tile.

**Stained-Glass Pillars**

## Stained-Glass Pillars

*shown on page 35*

### WHAT YOU NEED

Unscented candles
Rubbing alcohol
Paper towels
Flat black spray paint, such as Design Master
Paintbrushes
14kt gold paint
Acrylic paint in gold, green, sky blue, clay, red, metallic gold, eggplant, white, and/or other colors
Gold iridescent glaze, such as Delta

### HERE'S HOW

**1** Wipe unscented candle with rubbing alcohol and paper towels. Let dry. Spray-paint the candle with two coats of black paint, allowing to dry after each coat.

**2** Paint a border on candle using 14kt gold paint. Draw intersecting lines of gold paint between the borders to resemble a stained-glass window. Fill in sections with acrylic paints. Mix white with colors that are too dark, such as eggplant. Two to three coats of paint may be needed. Let dry after each coat.

**3** Brush on one coat of glaze. Let the glaze dry. Apply additional coats if desired. Let dry.

**Mosaic Tile Candles**

# handmade gifts to share

*Create sentimental gifts that will be remembered long after the holidays are past.*

HANDCRAFTED GIFTS ARE SPECIAL to make and to receive. **Very Merry Mugs**, *opposite*, are bright and cheery holders for candy, coffee, or hot cocoa. **Personalized Stemware Tags,** *above,* are welcome hostess gifts or party favors—and they're fun to make. Instructions are on page 54.

Peppery
Peach Sauce

Perfect served alongside cheese, drizzled over a mixed green salad, or splashed over roasted meats, **Peppery Peach Sauce,** *above*, is convenient to make from fresh or frozen peaches. **Holiday Surprise Bread,** *opposite*, blends the tastes of semisweet chocolate, candied cherries, and orange peel for a new winter morning favorite. Place a loaf on a pretty plate, and it's ready for gift giving. Recipes are on page 55.

To dress up bottles filled with liqueur, perfume, or bubble bath, **Bottle Baubles**, *opposite*, are dramatic touches that double as distinctive ornaments to hang from a Christmas tree. For everyone on your gift list who loves to display photos, tool **Magnetic Magic,** *above*. This stylish frame is crafted using an acrylic frame, aluminum, magnetic paint, and embossing tools. Photos are held in place with decorative pewter magnets. Instructions are on pages 56–57.

For a sweet-and-salty, no-cook topping, make several batches of **Honey-Nut Topping**, *above*. For giving, scoop it into a jar, top with a snowman lid, and tie on a pretty ribbon. For a cool snow-friend craft that will be used and appreciated all winter, cut out and stitch a **Sno-Cute Tote**, *opposite*, for the girls on your list. This soft character purse is a creative way to recycle outgrown or thrift-store sweaters. The recipe and instructions are on pages 57–58.

Stir up or whip up tasty and colorful **Marbled Mint Bark,**
*opposite*, to share with family and friends. Wrap up the candy
for giving in a box decorated with a trio of bottlebrush trees.
Share your talent for piecing and quilting with small projects
that go together quickly. Make a **Tree Hot Pad,** *above,* or a **Star
Hot Pad,** shown on page 60. These colorful designs will
brighten the kitchens of your favorite cooks. The recipe and
instructions are on pages 59–61.

Destined to become a holiday heirloom, this **Pretty Holly Pillow** can be created in hues to coordinate with any decor. Choose muted tones, *above*, or brighten the palette for contemporary appeal. White goes with everything, and that's just what they'll want to wear these lovely, soft mittens with—everything! Accented with pretty pearls, **Buttons and Beads Mittens,** *opposite*, will be appreciated when there's a nip in the air. Instructions are on pages 62–63.

## Very Merry Mugs

*shown on page 42*

### WHAT YOU NEED

- Wide masking tape
- Cutting mat or cutting surface
- Pencil
- Cup or other round object
- Crafts knife
- Clean white ceramic mugs; ruler
- Round stickers
- Acrylic enamel glass and ceramic
  paints, such as Pēbēo, in pink
  and green
- Wide paintbrush
- Small paintbrush handle
- Oven (optional)

**Personalized Stemware Tags.**

### HERE'S HOW

**1** To create scallops or zigzags around the top of the mug, lay a piece of wide masking tape on a cutting mat. Use a pencil to trace around a cup to make half-circles or a ruler to draw lines. Use a crafts knife to cut on the line. Place the tape around the mug.

**2** Apply stickers to mug for polka dots. Cut and apply small masking tape squares to mug for squares.

**3** Paint each mug, applying one color to the mug and a contrasting color to the handle. Paint over the tape and stickers and onto the surface of the mug using smooth, even strokes. Let the paint dry. Remove tape and stickers.

**4** To make tiny contrasting dots around the shapes, dip a paintbrush handle in paint; dot the paint onto the surface.

**5** Refer to the paint manufacturer's instructions and heat-set the paint in the oven if required.

## Personalized Stemware Tags

*shown on page 43*

### WHAT YOU NEED

- Tracing paper; pencil
- Vellum oval tags, such as
  Making Memories
- Transparency paper
- Black pen or computer and printer
- Adhesive laminate sheet
- Scissors
- Double-sided adhesive paper
- ⅛-inch hole punch
- ⅛-inch-wide silver ribbon

### HERE'S HOW

**1** To make a pattern, lay tracing paper over a vellum oval tag; trace the oval inside the trim.

**2** On the transparency paper, hand-write or print names to fit within the oval vellum tag.

**3** On the laminate sheet, cut out squares slightly larger than the tag size; apply the squares to the names on transparency paper. Holding the oval tag pattern beneath each name, cut out the shapes.

**4** Apply a square of double-sided adhesive paper to the back of the names. Cut off excess, peel off backing, and apply to the vellum tags.

**5** Punch a hole in each tag; attach silver ribbon through the hole. Use the ribbon to tie the tag to a stemmed glass.

**Very Merry Mugs**

**Peppery Peach Sauce**

*shown on page 44*

**WHAT YOU NEED**

- **4 pounds fresh peaches or three 16-ounce packages frozen unsweetened peach slices, thawed**
- **2 cups sugar**
- **1 5½-ounce can peach or apricot nectar**
- **¼ cup cider vinegar**
- **1 tablespoon lemon juice**
- **2 cloves garlic, minced**
- **1 fresh red chile pepper or habañero chile pepper, seeded and very finely chopped (about 1 tablespoon)\***
- **½ teaspoon salt**
- **1½ cups fresh raspberries**

**HERE'S HOW**

**1** Wash fresh peaches, if using. Peel and pit peaches. Place half of the fresh or frozen peaches in a food processor bowl or blender container. Cover and process or blend until peaches are very finely chopped. Transfer chopped peaches to a 6-quart Dutch oven. Repeat with remaining peaches. (You should have 5 cups chopped peaches.)

**2** Add sugar, nectar, vinegar, lemon juice, garlic, chile pepper, and salt to peaches in Dutch oven. Bring to boiling; reduce heat. Simmer, uncovered, for 15 to 20 minutes or until desired consistency, stirring occasionally. Remove from heat. Stir in raspberries.

**3** To process sauce in standard canning jars, follow the directions in Step 4. Or ladle sauce into decorative jars, cover and store in refrigerator up to 1 week.

**4** To process sauce, immediately ladle hot sauce into hot clean half-pint canning jars, leaving ¼-inch headspace. Wipe jar rims and adjust lids. Process jars in boiling-water canner 15 minutes (start timing when water begins to boil). Remove jars from canner; allow to cool. Stir sauce before serving. Makes 8 half-pint jars.

**5** To present as a gift, tie a ribbon around the jar. Label the jar with the contents and serving suggestions. Use a ribbon to tie a small spoon to the jar. *Chile peppers contain oils that can burn your skin and eyes. Avoid direct contact with them by wearing plastic or rubber gloves. If your bare hands touch the peppers, wash your hands well with soap and water.

**Holiday Surprise Bread**

*shown on page 45*

**WHAT YOU NEED**

- **3¾ to 4¼ cups all-purpose flour**
- **2 packages active dry yeast**
- **⅓ cup butter or margarine**
- **¾ cup milk**
- **⅓ cup sugar**
- **1 teaspoon salt**
- **2 eggs**
- **4 ounces semisweet chocolate, coarsely chopped (do not use semisweet chocolate pieces)**
- **¾ cup candied red cherries, chopped**
- **¼ cup diced candied orange peel**
- **2 teaspoons finely shredded orange peel**

**HERE'S HOW**

**1** In a large mixing bowl combine 1½ cups of the flour and the yeast. In a medium saucepan heat and stir butter, milk, sugar, and salt until warm (120°F to 130°F) and margarine almost melts. Add milk mixture and eggs to flour mixture. Beat with an electric mixer on low to medium speed for 30 seconds, scraping sides of bowl constantly. Beat on high speed for 3 minutes. Using a wooden spoon, stir in chocolate, cherries, candied orange peel, shredded orange peel, and as much of the remaining flour as you can.

**2** Turn dough out onto a lightly floured surface. Knead in enough of the remaining flour to make a moderately soft dough that is smooth and elastic (3 to 5 minutes total). Shape dough into a ball. Place in a lightly greased bowl; turn once to grease surface of dough. Cover; let rise in a warm place until double (1½ to 2 hours).

**3** Punch dough down. Turn dough out onto a lightly floured surface; divide in half. Cover; let rest for 10 minutes.

**4** Shape each portion of dough into a round loaf. Place on greased baking sheets. Press to flatten into 6-inch diameter rounds. Cover and let rise in a warm place until size nearly doubles (about 50 to 60 minutes).

**5** Using a sharp knife, cut an X about ½ inch deep in top of each loaf. Bake in a 325°F oven for 30 minutes or until loaves sound hollow when tapped. If necessary, cover loosely with foil the last 10 minutes of baking to prevent overbrowning. Remove from baking sheets and cool completely on wire racks. Makes 2 loaves (12 servings each).

**6** To present as a gift, wrap each cooled loaf in cellophane; place on a plate. Tie ribbon around the wrapped loaf and plate and tuck in an evergreen sprig.

**Holiday Surprise Bread**

## Bottle Baubles

*shown on page 46*

### WHAT YOU NEED

Wire snips
Gold fireplace screen; ruler
36-gauge aluminum tooling foil
36-gauge copper tooling foil
20-gauge copper wire
24-gauge gold wire
2-inch head pin
Silver seed beads
Clear acrylic faceted beads
6mm jump rings
Two 8-inch lengths of ball chain
4 ball chain ends
Tracing paper; pencil
Small sharp scissors
Embossing tool
1/8-inch hole punch, optional
Round-nose pliers
Needle-nose pliers
Strong adhesive, such as Goop
Small gold bead
Small silver spacer

### HERE'S HOW

**1** To make the diamond-shape bauble, use wire snips to cut a 3-inch square from fireplace screen. From aluminum tooling foil, use scissors to cut a 1¼-inch square. On tracing paper write "Joy." Place the tracing wrong side down on the back side of the aluminum square. Use the embossing tool to trace the word (in reverse) and to dot the edges of the square. Punch a hole in each corner of the square. Run copper wire through the punched holes to attach the aluminum square on the screen square.

**2** Thread seed beads and acrylic faceted bead onto a head pin. Bend wire end using round-nose pliers. Using needle-nose pliers and a jump ring, attach the beaded head pin to the screen square.

**3** Attach ball chain ends to ball chain. Use needle-nose pliers and jump rings to attach chain to screen square.

**4** To make the round bauble, trace a 2¼-inch circle on aluminum using an embossing tool; cut out with scissors.

Bottle Baubles

On the copper foil trace a 1½-inch circle using an embossing tool; cut out with scissors. From fireplace screen, use wire snips to cut two squares.

**5** On the back side of the aluminum circle, emboss perpendicular lines around the edge. On the back side of the copper circle, emboss dots around the edge. Lay one screen square in the center of the copper circle and emboss dots in a spoke pattern around the square. Use adhesive to secure one screen square to the front of the copper circle and one edge of the screen square to the back side of the aluminum circle. Let the adhesive dry.

**6** Layer the circles and punch two small holes through the layers in the middle of the screen square. Thread a length of gold wire through a gold bead, a silver spacer, a clear faceted bead, and through the holes in the bauble. Twist wires together to secure.

**7** Attach ball chain ends to ball chain. Use needle-nose pliers and jump rings to attach chain to screen.

## Magnetic Magic

*shown on page 47*

### WHAT YOU NEED

Lightweight aluminum sheet, such
   as ArtEmboss
5×7 acrylic photo frame; scissors
Foam-core board or cardboard
Masking tape; double-sided tape
Pewter adornment pieces
Wood-embossing tool
Stylus-embossing tool
Ballpoint pen; decorative template,
   such as American Traditional
   Stencils in Braided Borders
Silver scrapbook paper
Magnetic wall paint
Acrylic paints in silver and black
Paintbrush
½-inch round, strong magnets
Strong adhesive, such as
   Quick Grip
Paper towels; 5×7-inch photograph

### HERE'S HOW

**1** Mark and cut aluminum to fit the front of the frame. Place aluminum on foam board; tape a pewter adornment to the underside of a corner. Use the wood-embossing tool to gently rub an impression of the adornment. Trace the outer edges with the stylus tool to further accent the design. Repeat process for each corner of the aluminum.

**2** On the back of the aluminum, use a ballpoint pen to trace the border stencil. Emboss dots in the metal along the edge of the tooled design.

**3** Use double-sided tape to adhere the tooled metal to the acrylic frame. Cut a piece of silver paper to fit inside acrylic frame to cover the back of tooled metal.

**4** Follow the directions from the magnetic paint manufacturer to paint the tooled metal frame. Let the paint dry. Brush on a coat of acrylic silver paint over the magnetic paint; let dry. Use a paper towel to rub black acrylic paint on the silver paint; wipe off excess paint. Let the paint dry.

**5** Glue adornments to magnets using strong adhesive; let dry. Attach a photo to the frame using the magnets.

Honey-Nut Topping

## Honey-Nut Topping

*shown on page 48*

### WHAT YOU NEED for the topping

  **1**  **10-ounce can mixed nuts (without peanuts)**
**1¼**  **cups honey**
 **⅓**  **cup maple syrup**

### HERE'S HOW

**1** In a bowl combine nuts, honey, and maple syrup. Stir until nuts are coated.

**2** Spoon nut mixture into three clean, dry half-pint jars. Cover and store at room temperature for up to 3 weeks. Serve the topping over cereal, pound cake, fresh fruit, or ice cream. Makes 3 half-pint jars of topping.

### WHAT YOU NEED for the jar

Jar with wooden lid
Drill and bit
2½-inch-long stove bolt and nut
Newspapers
Silver-blue spray paint
White air-dry clay, such as Crayola Model Magic
Flat toothpicks
Scissors
Paintbrush
Acrylic paints in black, orange, and white
¼-inch-wide ribbon for scarf
Glitter glaze
1-inch-wide ribbon for jar
Plastic wrap

### HERE'S HOW

**1** In the center of the jar lid, drill a hole large enough to accommodate the bolt.

**2** In a well-ventilated work area, cover the work surface with newspapers. Spray-paint the outside of the lid silver-blue. Let the paint dry.

**3** Insert the bolt through the bottom of the lid; place the nut on the bolt. The bolt will protrude from the lid top.

**4** Use three balls of clay to shape a snowman approximately 3 inches high. Press the clay snowman onto the stove bolt. To form a hat, shape a flat, quarter-size brim. Shape a hat top and press to the brim. Press hat to snowman. Roll a carrot shape for the nose. Break off 1 inch from a toothpick; press one end into the carrot nose and the opposite end into the snowman. For snowman arms, use scissors to cut slits into wide ends of two toothpicks; press uncut ends into the snowman. Let the clay dry.

**5** Paint the hat black. Paint the nose orange. Paint the arms a mix of white and black. To make eyes, mouth, and buttons, dip the handle end of a paintbrush into paint; dot the paint onto the snowman. Let the paint dry.

**6** Tie a ribbon scarf on the snowman. Coat the snowman and lid with glitter glaze. Let dry. Tie a ribbon around the neck of the jar. Top the jar with plastic wrap before turning on the painted lid.

Magnetic Magic

## Sno-Cute Tote

*shown on page 49*

### WHAT YOU NEED

Tracing paper; pencil; scissors
Old white cotton knit sweater
Fleece for hat and scarf
Lining fabric; iron-on batting
Orange felt for nose; iron
Needle; thread; poly-fil stuffing
Sewing machine; powder blush
Black yarn for eyes and mouth

### HERE'S HOW

**1** Enlarge and trace the patterns, *below* and *opposite*. Cut corresponding pieces from sweater, fleece, and iron-on batting. For handle, use the longest length possible from sweater back and cut a 2½-inch strip. Cut the same length from iron-on batting.

**2** Iron on batting to back sides of the purse sweater pieces.

**3** Sew with ¼-inch seams. Stitch the hat fleece back to the purse back sweater piece. Sew scarf fringe piece to the right side of the front sweater piece with piece pointing up. Stitch scarf to bottom of purse sweater front, right sides together, over fringe piece.

**4** Sew nose pieces together, right sides facing, leaving short, straight edge open. Turn right side out; stuff with small piece of poly-fil stuffing. Sew onto front of purse sweater piece, stitching by hand with matching thread. Use the stitch diagrams, *opposite*, as guides. Sew the eyes and mouth with fine yarn, stitching four French knots clustered together for eyes and two French knots at ends of mouth. Chain-stitch the mouth.

**5** With right sides together, stitch the top straight seam of front lining to the purse front. Flip the lining over so that the wrong sides are together, bottom and side edges are even, and front folds over ⅜ inch to the back side of the front. Baste around the side and bottom edges.

**6** Wrong sides together, baste lining to back purse section. Baste down sides and bottom leaving hat part free.

**Sno-Cute Tote**

**7** Right sides together, stitch the front purse and lining to the back and lining.

**8** With right sides together, stitch the hat lining to the hat piece of purse back, sewing the side edges and top slant only. Turn the hat right side out. Turn the purse right side out.

**9** Stitch in seam at bottom edge of hat where it is joined to the purse back piece, catching in the hat lining on the inside.

**10** Sew the handle, right sides together, down the long edge. Turn right side out.

Sew the handle to the sides of the purse, stitching straight across handle through all layers.

**11** For the scarf fringe, cut up every ¼ inch to within ¾ inches of seam. Pull on the lengths to stretch and curl the fleece.

**12** For hat fringe, cut every ¼ inch up from unsewn straight edge. Pull together in a bunch and tie with a ¼×10-inch piece of fleece.

**13** Dust cheeks with blush.

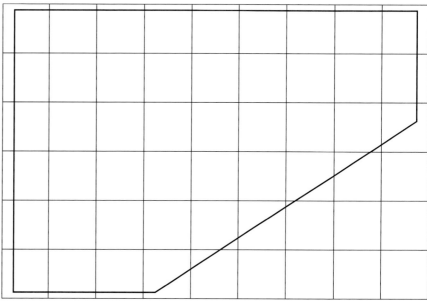

**Sno-Cute Tote—Hat
reproduce at 200%**

1 square = 1 inch

**Chain Stitch**

**French Knot**

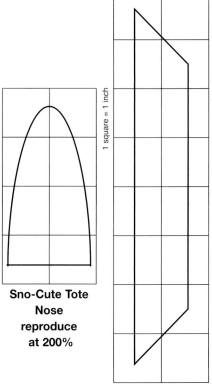

**Sno-Cute Tote
Nose
reproduce
at 200%**

1 square = 1 inch

**Sno-Cute Tote
Scarf
reproduce
at 200%**

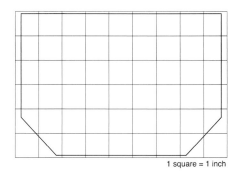

1 square = 1 inch

**Sno-Cute Tote—Purse
reproduce at 400%**

**Marbled Mint Bark**

## Marbled Mint Bark

*shown on page 50*

### WHAT YOU NEED for the Marbled Mint Bark

- 1 **pound vanilla-flavored candy coating, cut up into small pieces**
- ¾ **cup finely crushed red and/or green striped round peppermint candies**
  **Red food coloring, optional**
- ⅓ **cup semisweet chocolate pieces**

### HERE'S HOW

**1** Line a baking sheet with aluminum foil; set aside.

**2** In a microwave-safe 4-cup glass measure, microwave candy coating on 100% power (high) for 2 to 3 minutes, stirring after every minute. Stir in crushed candies and, if desired, red food coloring. Pour candy mixture onto prepared baking sheet to approximately ¼-inch thickness.

**3** In a glass measuring cup, microwave chocolate pieces on 100% power for 1 to 2 minutes or until soft enough to stir smooth, stirring after 1 minute. Drizzle chocolate over candy mixture. Gently zigzag a narrow metal spatula through the chocolate and peppermint layers to marble.

**4** Let candy stand several hours or until firm. Or chill about 30 minutes or until firm. Use foil to lift candy from baking sheet; carefully break candy into pieces. Store candy, tightly covered, at room temperature up to 2 weeks. Makes about 1¼ pounds candy.

### WHAT YOU NEED for the wrap

White box with lid
3 small bottlebrush trees with bases
Thick white crafts glue
Wood stars
Yellow acrylic paint; paintbrush
Red raffia
Tissue paper, waxed paper, or parchment paper
Scissors

### HERE'S HOW

**1** Arrange and glue the bases of the trees to the box lid. Let the glue dry.

**2** Paint the stars yellow. Let dry. Glue a star to the top of each tree. Let dry.

**3** Tie raffia on the trees below the stars; trim the ends. Line the box with tissue paper; fill the box with Marbled Mint Bark.

## Star Hot Pad

*shown at right*

### WHAT YOU NEED for star hot pad

Template paper; pencil; ⅛ yard *each* gold, blue, and cream print fabrics
¼ yard blue fabric for backing and binding; scissors
Lightweight batting; pins
Sewing machine; thread; needle
#5 yellow and blue pearl cotton
½-inch cabone ring; crochet hook

### HERE'S HOW

**1** Adding ¼-inch seam allowances to each edge, make templates from the patterns, *opposite*. From fabric cut the following:

A—1 gold square
B—8 gold triangles
C—4 blue triangles
D—4 blue squares
E—4 cream print triangles
F—8 blue triangles
G—4 cream print squares

**2** Refer to the diagram, *opposite*, for the Star Hot Pad and to Step 2 and Step 3 for the Tree Hot Pad to layer, tie, and bind the Star Hot Pad, and to attach the cabone ring for a hanger.

## Tree Hot Pad

*shown on page 51*

### WHAT YOU NEED for tree hot pad

Template paper; pencil
⅛ yard *each* green, green print, white, and red fabrics
Scrap of brown fabric
¼ yard red fabric for backing and binding
Scissors; pins; lightweight batting
Thread; needle; sewing machine
#5 red pearl cotton
½-inch cabone ring; crochet hook

### HERE'S HOW

**1** Adding a ¼-inch seam allowance to each edge, make templates from the patterns, *opposite*. From fabric cut the following:

A—3 green print squares
B—3 green trapezoids
C—3 green trapezoids
D—3 green print triangles
E—4 white triangles
F—2 red triangles
G—1 brown tree trunk
H—2 white triangles

**2** Refer to the diagrams, *opposite*, to piece the hot pad. Cut the backing 2 inches larger all around than the pieced top. Cut batting slightly larger. Layer the backing, batting, and top; pin the edges. Tie through all layers, as shown on page 61, using the pearl cotton.

**3** Fold the backing fabric to the top, turning under the raw edges, to create a binding. Hand-stitch the binding to the top. Single-crochet around a cabone ring with pearl cotton; hand-stitch it to a corner of the hot pad for hanging.

**Star Hot Pad**

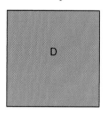

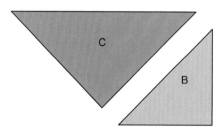

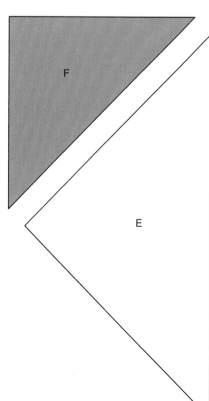

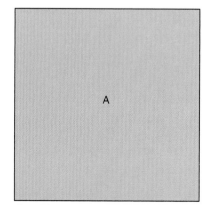

**Star Hot Pad Pattern**

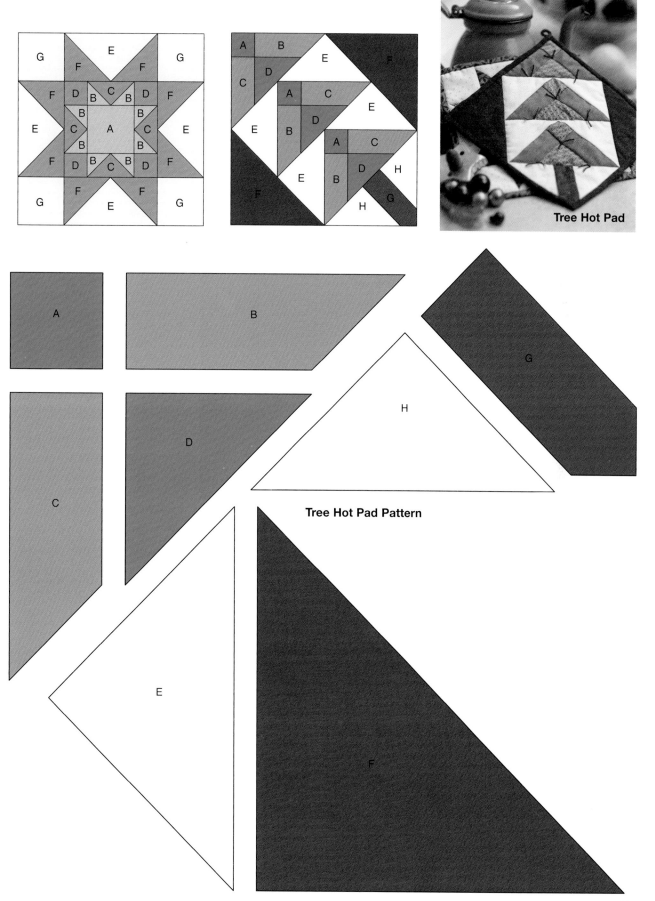

Tree Hot Pad

Tree Hot Pad Pattern

## Pretty Holly Pillow
*shown on page 52*

### WHAT YOU NEED
1¼ yards of 54-inch-wide gold
    moiré decorator fabric
Scissors; ruler; 1½-inch donut bead
1 yard of 1½-inch-wide ribbon
4 yards of ⅜-inch-wide ribbon
16-inch square pillow form
⅛ yard of gold imitation suede fabric
Fusible transweb paper
Press cloth; fabric glue
Metallic gold machine thread
Nine ½-inch red beads
Pink powder blush

### HERE'S HOW
**1** From moiré cut two 17-inch squares
for the pillow front and back. Also from
moiré cut and piece enough 3-inch-
wide strips to equal a 144-inch
continuous loop for the ruffle.

**2** Refer to photo and center donut bead
under one length of wide ribbon. Weave
a second length of ribbon through bead,
catching first ribbon. Baste the ribbon
ends to the edges of the pillow front.

**3** Wrong sides together, fold the ruffle
loop in half lengthwise, matching raw
edges; lightly press. Sew the narrow
ribbon close to, but not on, the fold.
Along the raw edge of the ruffle, stitch
gathering threads. Mark the ruffle to
make four equal sections; match the
marks to the center of each side of the
pillow front, raw edges even and
ribbon-trimmed side toward the pillow
front. Pull up gathering threads, pin,
and sew the ruffle to the pillow front,
using a scant ½-inch seam allowance.

**4** Right sides facing, sew pillow front to
back with a ½-inch seam allowance;
leave an opening for turning. Trim the
corners. Turn to right side. Insert pillow
form and stitch the opening closed.

**5** Trace five holly leaves on fusible
transweb paper. Using a press cloth, fuse
leaves to wrong side of imitation suede.
Cut out leaves; remove paper backing.

**6** Machine-satin-stitch (close zigzag)
leaf veins with metallic gold thread,

**Pretty Holly Pillow**

stretching the leaf slightly to shape.
Glue leaves to the pillow front. Cluster
and glue beads for berries. Apply blush
to the leaves.

## Buttons and Beads Mittens
*shown on page 53*

**SKILL LEVEL:** Intermediate

**SIZE:** Child size 6–8 (10–12);
Adult size medium

**FINISHED MEASUREMENTS:**
Width: 3¼" (3½", 3¾")
Length: 7½" (9", 10")

### WHAT YOU NEED
Lion Brand, Wool-Ease Chunky,
    Article #630, 80% acrylic/20%
    wool yarn (153 yards per ball):
    1 ball of Tinsel White (301)
Size 6 (4.25mm) knitting needles or
    size needed to obtain gauge
2 ring-type stitch markers
Yarn needle; 8mm pearl beads
6 decorative pearl buttons
Sewing needle and white thread

### ABBREVIATIONS:
est = established
k = knit
m = make 1 stitch
p = purl
pm = place marker
rep = repeat
rnd(s) = round(s)
RS = right side
sl = slip
st(s) = stitch(es)
St st = stockinette stitch
tog = together
WS = wrong side

### STITCHES USED:
Diamond (over 7 sts; a rep of 8 rows)
**Row 1 (RS):** P1.
**Row 2 and each following WS row:**
Knit the k sts and purl the p sts as
they appear.
**Row 3:** P1, k1, p1.
**Row 5:** P1, k3, p1.
**Row 7:** P1, k5, p1.
**Row 8:** As Row 2.
Rep Rows 1–8 for 3 total times, then rep
Rows 1–2 again.

## INSTRUCTIONS—RIGHT MITTEN
### SHORT SIDE OF VENT
Wind a small ball of yarn. Cast on 8 sts.
**Row 1 (WS):** Purl.
**Row 2:** K1, p1; (k3, p1), k2.
**Row 3:** (P1, k1) across.
**Row 4:** Rep Row 2.
**Row 5:** Rep Row 1.
Place these 8 sts onto a spare needle; set aside.

### LONG SIDE OF VENT
With the big ball of yarn, cast on 24 sts.
**Row 1:** Purl.
**Row 2:** K1, p1; (k3, p1) across, ending k2.
**Row 3:** (P1, k1) across.
**Row 4:** Rep Row 2.
**Row 5:** Rep Row 1.

### JOINING SIDES
Purl across 24 sts, then purl 8 sts from holder (cut yarn, leaving a tail to weave in later). K across, dec 5 (3, 1) st—27 (29, 31) sts. Beginning with a purl row, work 1 (3, 5) St st rows (knit RS rows, purl WS rows).

### BODY PATTERN
K6 (7, 7), pl for first Diamond row, k to end. Pattern is now set. Work even to approximately 2" (2½", 3") from beg, ending with a WS row.

### THUMB
**Note:** To make 1 stitch (m1); lift the horizontal bar between right and left needles onto the left needle, and k into back of this loop.
**Row 1 (RS):** Work 13 (14, 15) sts, pm, M1, k1, M1, pm, work to end of row.
**Row 2:** Pattern across.
**Row 3:** Work to marker, sl marker, M1, k to marker, M1, sl marker, work to end of row.
Rep Rows 2–3 until there are 11 (13, 13) sts between markers. P 1 row. Next Row: Pattern across, removing markers and placing thumb sts onto a spare strand of yarn. Continue est pattern on the 26 (28, 30) sts until piece measures approximately 7 (8, 9)" from beg, ending with a WS row, placing marker after 13th (14th, 15th) st.

### TOP SHAPING
**Note:** Ssk—Slip next 2 sts knitwise, one at a time to right-hand needle;

**Buttons and Beads Mittens**

insert tip of left-hand needle into fronts of these 2 sts and k tog.
**Row 1 (RS):** Ssk, pattern across to 2 sts before marker, k2tog, sl marker, ssk, k to last 2 sts, k2tog.
**Row 2:** Pattern across.
Rep Rows 1–2 until 18 (20, 18) sts rem, ending with Row 2. (K2tog) across. P9 (10, 9). Leaving a long tail for sewing, cut yarn.

### CLOSURE
Thread tail into yarn needle. Beginning with the last st on needle, take yarn back through rem sts, twice. Pull up to tightly close opening. Leave tail for sewing.

### THUMB
With RS facing, return sts to needle. Join yarn and k11 (13, 13). P4 (5, 5), p2tog, p5 (6, 6). Work 4 (6, 6) more rows. (K2tog) across. Cut yarn, leaving a 10" tail. Rep Closure as for Top. Join thumb seam. Darn opening. Weave in loose ends on WS of fabric.

### FINISHING
With the RS facing, pick up and k 23 sts along long lower edge, 5 sts along first side of vent, 5 sts along 2nd side of vent, and 7 sts along short lower edge. Bind off knitwise and loosely.

Sew one bead in the center of each diamond along lower edge and one button in each diamond on back side of mitten. Join sides.

### LEFT MITTEN
Make a Long Side as for Right Mitten and save sts on a spare needle. Make a Short Side as for Right Mitten. Purl across 8 sts then purl across 24 sts. K across, dec 5 (3, 1) sts—27 (29, 31) sts. Beginning with a purl row, work 1 (3, 5) St st row(s).

### BODY PATTERN
K20 (21, 23) sts, p1 for first Diamond row, k to end. Pattern is now set. Complete as for the Right Mitten to Finishing.

### FINISHING
With RS facing, pick up and k7 sts along short lower edge, 5 sts along first side of vent, 5 sts along second side of vent, and 23 sts along long lower edge. Complete as for Right Mitten.

# wondrous wreaths

*Enhance holiday decorating with creatively made wreaths in a variety of styles.*

FASHION WREATHS THAT REFLECT the beauty of the season. **Jingling Nature Wreath,** *above*, has bright bands of gold jingle bells nestled among petite pinecones. **Nature's Best,** *opposite*, can be made using leaves and nuts collected from an autumn walk in the woods. Instructions are on page 74.

For a fresh twist using traditional holiday motifs, craft wreaths that step beyond evergreen. Vintage Button Wreath, *above*, is a visual treat that will last for years. Hundreds of pearly buttons are accented with wide velvet and silvery sprigs for contrast. Beribboned Beauty, *opposite*, is a striking combination of silver and red—an elegant way to greet visitors. Clusters of shiny bows and bright ornaments attach to a wreath form quickly and easily. Instructions are on pages 74–75.

*Buttons and bows give holiday wreaths contemporary flair.*

Add naturally bright color to a fresh evergreen wreath with **Apples All Around.** Instructions are on page 75.

Make a fresh green wreath extraordinary with purchased trims. Attach ornaments for Star Appeal, *above*, or a strap of large, ornate jingle bells for a Sleigh Bell Surprise, *below*. Instructions are on pages 75–76.

Choose unexpected trims to add subtle or contrasting color
and texture to evergreen wreaths. In Fruits and Feathers,
*above*, vivid peacock feathers and glistening beaded fruit
nestle among fresh greenery. Evergreen and Grapes, *opposite*,
is a simple but striking pairing of realistic-looking grapes and
silvery-blue evergreen boughs. For wreaths that last longer
than one season, use bases of artificial greenery. Instructions
are on pages 76–77.

For a rustic wreath, craft A Natural Winner, *opposite*, by tying together twigs and branches. Clip glass bird ornaments to a couple of branch perches for a colorful accent. Starry Stable, *above*, made from a picture-frame base, is layered with wooden stars painted silver and gold. An evergreen roof drapes gracefully across the top and sides of the wreath, and a simple purple bow provides a royal finish. Instructions are on page 77.

**Jingling Nature Wreath**

## Jingling Nature Wreath

*shown on page 64*

**WHAT YOU NEED**

18-inch piece of crafting wire
Plastic foam wreath form
Hot-glue gun and glue sticks
Moss; gold jingle bells
Petite pinecones

**HERE'S HOW**

**1** Wrap wire around wreath form and create a loop for hanging. Hot-glue moss to the top and sides of the form.
**2** Mark four equally spaced divisions on the moss-covered wreath. Glue three rows of bells along each mark. Glue the petite pinecones in the spaces between the rows of bells.

## Nature's Best

*shown on page 65*

**WHAT YOU NEED**

18-inch piece of crafting wire
Plastic foam wreath form
Brown wide wired ribbon
Straight pins
Hot-glue gun and glue sticks
Assorted nuts, buckeyes, dried
   flowers, artificial berries, etc.
Newspapers; dried, pressed leaves
Metallic gold spray paint
Transparent spray paints in yellow
   and red, such as Krylon glass
   paints or automotive and
   hobby paint

**Nature's Best**

**HERE'S HOW**

**1** Wrap wire around wreath form and create a loop for hanging. Wrap and pin the ribbon around the wreath form.
**2** Hot-glue nuts and dried materials to the wreath in circles.
**3** In a well-ventilated work area, cover surface with newspapers. Lay dried pressed leaves on newspapers. Spray-paint the leaves gold. Let them dry. Spray transparent paints over the gold. Let dry. Arrange and hot-glue the leaf stems to the back of the wreath to surround the nuts and dried materials.

## Vintage Button Wreath

*shown on page 66*

**WHAT YOU NEED**

Hot-glue gun and glue sticks
Straw wreath form
White grosgrain ribbon
½-inch old and new white buttons
3-inch-wide red velvet ribbon
Scissors
Dried flowers

**HERE'S HOW**

**1** Wrap and glue the white ribbon to cover the wreath.
**2** Glue rows of buttons on the ribbon to cover the wreath.
**3** For the hanger, tie the red ribbon through the wreath; trim the ends. Slip dried flowers through the opening in the ribbon.

**Vintage Button Wreath**

## Beribboned Beauty

*shown on page 67*

**WHAT YOU NEED**

Plastic foam wreath form
Silver ribbon in various shades,
    textures, and widths
Thick white crafts glue; floral wire
Wire snips; scissors
Metal floral picks
Red wire-edged ribbon
Hot-glue gun and glue sticks
Small red ornament cluster picks

**HERE'S HOW**

**1** Wrap the wreath form with a length of silver ribbon; glue to secure.
**2** Cut and loop silver ribbons, attach to floral picks, and insert the picks in the wreath to fully cover most of the wreath, allowing space for the red ribbon loops and streamers.
**3** Cut red ribbon loops and wire to picks. Insert the loops and two long streamers in the wreath using the photo, *below*, as a guide. Glue as needed.
**4** Arrange ornament clusters between silver ribbons, gluing as needed.

**5** Cut wire 18 inches long, thread it through the top of the wreath and twist the wire to shape a hanging loop.

Apples All Around

## Apples All Around

*shown on page 68*

**WHAT YOU NEED**

Heavy-gauge copper or armature
    wire
Evergreen wreath
Apples
Floral wire
3×48-inch strip of gingham
Spray starch; iron

**HERE'S HOW**

**1** Shape flexible heavy-gauge copper or armature wire into a circle to fit on the wreath front.
**2** Skewer apples with the ring of wire, securing wire ends in an apple. Secure the ring of apples to the wreath with floral wire, wrapping between apples.
**3** Stiffen the gingham strip with spray starch and an iron. Tie it in a bow with tails and wire it to the wreath. The wreath may last up to two weeks.

Star Appeal

## Star Appeal

*shown on page 69*

**WHAT YOU NEED**

Gold beaded wire
2 large and 3 small transparent
    shiny star ornaments
Evergreen wreath
Hot-glue gun and glue sticks or
    green floral wire
Scissors
8 yards of ¼-inch-wide ribbon in
    white or silver
Ruler

**HERE'S HOW**

**1** Wrap beaded wire around the small stars. Arrange the stars in a cluster on the wreath.
**2** Glue or use lengths of green floral wire to secure the stars to the wreath.
**3** Cut the ribbon into 1-yard lengths. Tie the ribbons to the wreath, allowing long tails. Slightly curl or twist the ribbon tails and arrange them among the greenery and stars.

Beribboned Beauty

## Sleigh Bell Surprise

*shown on page 69*

**WHAT YOU NEED**

Scissors; yardstick
2-inch-wide red plaid ribbon
Sleigh bells on leather strap
Crafting wire
Evergreen wreath with assorted
    greenery and berries

**HERE'S HOW**

**1** Cut two 36-inch lengths of ribbon. With the ribbons layered, lay one end of the sleigh bell strap on the ribbon and tie the ribbon into a bow around the leather strap. Trim the long ribbon tails.
**2** Use crafting wire to wrap and secure the sleigh bell strap diagonally across the wreath. Arrange the ribbon tails across the wreath.

## Fruits and Feathers

*shown on page 70*

**WHAT YOU NEED**

Crafting wire
Beaded grapes

**Evergreen and Grapes**

Metal needlepoint ring (available in
    crafts stores) to fit the wreath
Evergreen wreath; beaded apple
Hot-glue gun and glue sticks
Peacock feathers

**HERE'S HOW**

**1** Wire clusters of beaded grapes to the needlepoint ring, spacing the clusters to allow room for the beaded apples after the grapes are attached to the wreath.

**2** Center the grape cluster ring on the evergreen wreath and wire it in place. To hold the beaded apples in place, apply a generous amount of hot glue on the ring and surrounding greens. Lay the beaded apples in the glue to secure them.

**3** Insert peacock feathers around the ring and hot-glue them in place.

**Sleigh Bell Surprise**

**Fruits and Feathers**

## Evergreen and Grapes

*shown on page 71 and 76*

**WHAT YOU NEED**

Floral wire
Artificial champagne grape clusters
14-inch 4-wire box wreath form
Branch clippers
Fresh pine, spruce, and cedar
   greenery

**HERE'S HOW**

**1** Wire the artificial grape clusters to the innermost wire circle of the wreath form, packing the grapes tightly until the inner band is 2 to 3 inches wide and solidly packed.
**2** From the assorted fresh greenery, clip small branches and insert the woody ends between the wires of the wreath form as shown, *opposite*, to secure them with florist's wire.

## A Natural Winner

*shown on page 72*

**WHAT YOU NEED**

48 to 64 straight twigs and
   branches, at least 10 inches
   long and about ¼ to ½-inch in
   diameter
Florist's wire
Twine
Hot-glue gun and glue sticks
Perennial sprigs, such as spirea
Clip-on bird ornaments
1 yard of 2-inch-wide ribbon
Ruler; scissors

**HERE'S HOW**

**1** Gather twigs and branches into eight bundles, keeping lengths slightly uneven for a natural appearance. Wire the bundles together about 3 inches from each end.
**2** Lay four of the bundles in a square. Intersect the square with four bundles to

**Starry Stable**

create an octagon. Wire the bundles together at each intersection as shown in the photo, *left*.
**3** Cut 18- to 24-inch lengths of twine to wrap around each wired intersection to conceal wire. Glue twine ends to secure.
**4** Insert perennial sprigs. Clip bird ornaments to the wreath. Loop ribbon through the wreath for a hanger.

## Starry Stable

*shown on page 73*

**WHAT YOU NEED**

Unfinished wood frame
Acrylic paints in white, silver, and
   gold; paintbrush
Wood stars in 2 sizes
Medium-grit sandpaper
Hot-glue gun and glue sticks
Fresh greenery
2-inch-wide purple wire-edged
   ribbon; scissors; fresh greenery
Floral wire; ruler

**HERE'S HOW**

**1** Paint the frame white. Paint large stars silver and small stars gold. Let the paint dry.
**2** Lightly sand the frame to give it a rustic appearance.
**3** Use hot glue to layer and adhere the stars to bottom and sides of the frame.
**4** Cut a 36-inch length of ribbon; wire it to the side of the frame without stars. Wire greenery to cascade across the top and sides. Use wire to hang the wreath.

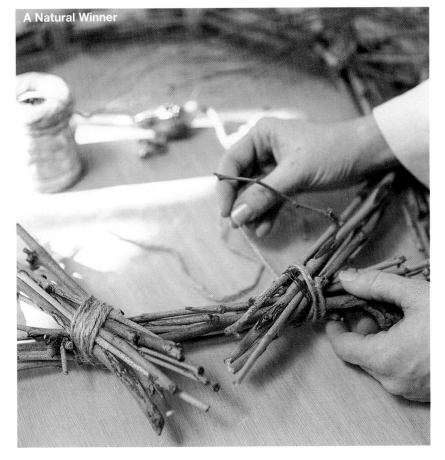

**A Natural Winner**

# sweet treats

*'Tis the season for extravagant cookies,
candies, and other delectable desserts.*

BE READY FOR GATHERINGS of family and friends
with these holiday sweets. **Citrus Snowflakes,**
buttery cookies with hints of lemon and lime,
*opposite,* rival the beauty of nature's winter crystals.
When you have carolers calling, treat them to a
plateful of **Key Lime Fudge,** *above.* Recipes and gift
box instructions are on page 86.

Say "Happy Holidays" with a homemade gift. A decorated box or pretty tin filled to the brim with freshly baked cookies is a heartwarming present. **Peanut Butter Fudge Tartlets,** *above*, are the quintessential Santa treat, too! The **Coconut-Cashew Pralines,** *opposite*, enticing Southern-inspired sweets, get a new twist using cashews and coconut—they're quite possibly more irresistible than the original! For fancy presentation, place the pralines in holiday candy papers and arrange them on a colorful plate. The recipes are on page 87.

Extraordinary fruit-filled creations, Christmas Biscotti, *opposite*, is filled with dried cranberries and pistachios for seasonal taste and beautiful color. To present the biscotti, make and decorate the cutout-tree gift bag. Braided Cranberry Bread with a Twist, *above*, is the perfectly stunning holiday bread that will be requested again and again for breakfast, teatime, or snacks. Recipes and gift bag instructions are on page 88.

Come in from the cold to enjoy warm-from-the-oven **Holiday Snowmen,** *above*. Kids will love making, decorating, and eating these shapely cookies—a cozy way to spend a wintry afternoon. Plain, frosted, or dressed in gumdrops, these treats are sure to be memory-makers. **Snickerdoodle Pinwheels,** *opposite*, are a creative spin on the traditional cookie that's good year-round. Cinnamon is spiraled through the dough rather than sprinkled on top. Recipes are on page 89.

## Citrus Snowflakes

*shown on page 78*

**WHAT YOU NEED for the cookies**
 ½   **cup butter, softened**
 ⅓   **cup shortening**
 1   **cup granulated sugar**
 ⅓   **cup sour cream**
 1   **egg**
 1   **teaspoon vanilla**
 2   **teaspoons finely shredded lemon peel**
 ½   **teaspoon finely shredded lime peel**
 ¾   **teaspoon baking powder**
 ¼   **teaspoon baking soda**
    **Dash salt**
 2½   **cups all-purpose flour**
    **Pearl sugar, fine sanding sugar, coarse sugar, and/or white edible glitter**
    **Sifted powdered sugar, optional**

**1** In a large mixing bowl beat butter and shortening with an electric mixer on medium to high speed for 30 seconds.
**2** Add granulated sugar, sour cream, egg, vanilla, lemon and lime peels, baking powder, baking soda, and salt. Beat until combined, scraping sides of bowl occasionally. Beat in as much of the flour as you can with the mixer. Stir in any remaining flour with a wooden spoon.

Divide dough in half. Cover and chill about 2 hours or until easy to handle.
**3** On a lightly floured surface roll half of the dough at a time to ⅛- to ¼-inch thickness. Use assorted snowflake cookie cutters or a sharp knife dipped in flour to cut dough into snowflake shapes. On the cutouts use hors d'oeuvre cutters or straws to cut designs that resemble snowflakes; use a straw to flute the edges. Using a wide spatula, place cookies about 1 inch apart on an ungreased cookie sheet. If desired, sprinkle with various sugars or glitter.
**4** Bake in a 375°F oven for 7 to 8 minutes or until edges are firm and bottoms are very light brown. Transfer cookies to a wire rack to cool. If desired, sprinkle cooled cookies with powdered sugar. Store in a tightly covered container at room temperature for up to 3 days or in the freezer up to 3 months. Makes about forty 2½-inch cookies.

**WHAT YOU NEED for the gift box**
    Small white box, approximately 8 inches square
    White paint pen
    White glitter
    Cellophane

**HERE'S HOW**
**1** On the box lid, use the paint pen to draw several six-pointed crosses for basic snowflake shapes.
**2** Using the paint pen, make tiny lines or dots on the snowflake shapes and between the snowflakes.
**3** While the paint is wet, sprinkle glitter onto the snowflakes. Let the glitter set.
**4** Use cellophane to line box, allowing ample cellophane to extend over the sides. Place cookies in the box, wrap cellophane to cover the cookies. Cover with the decorated box lid.

## Key Lime Fudge

*shown on page 79*

**WHAT YOU NEED for the fudge**
 3   **cups white baking pieces**
 1¼   **cups sweetened condensed milk**
 2   **teaspoons finely shredded lime peel**
 2   **tablespoons bottled Key lime juice or regular lime juice**
 1   **cup chopped macadamia nuts, toasted if desired**

**HERE'S HOW**
**1** Line an 8×8×2-inch or 9×9×2-inch baking pan with foil, extending foil over edges of pan. Butter foil; set aside.
**2** In a large, heavy saucepan stir baking pieces and sweetened condensed milk over low heat just until pieces are melted and mixture is smooth. Remove from heat. Stir in lime peel and lime juice. Stir in macadamia nuts.
**3** Spread mixture evenly into the prepared pan. If desired, sprinkle a few additional coarsely chopped macadamia nuts over the top. Cover and chill for 2 hours or until firm.
**4** Lift fudge from pan using edges of foil. Peel off foil. Cut into pieces. Store in an airtight container at room temperature for up to 1 week or in the freezer for up to 2 months. Makes 2½ pounds fudge or 80 pieces.

## Peanut Butter-Fudge Tartlets

*shown on page 80*

### WHAT YOU NEED

- ½ **cup butter, softened**
- ½ **cup peanut butter**
- ½ **cup granulated sugar**
- ½ **cup packed brown sugar or ¼ cup honey**
- ½ **teaspoon baking soda**
- ½ **teaspoon baking powder**
- 1 **egg**
- ½ **teaspoon vanilla**
- 1½ **cups all-purpose flour**
- ½ **cup semisweet chocolate pieces**
- ¼ **cup sweetened condensed milk**

### HERE'S HOW

**1** In a large mixing bowl beat butter and peanut butter with an electric mixer on medium to high speed for 30 seconds. Add the granulated sugar, brown sugar, baking soda, and baking powder. Beat until combined, scraping sides of bowl occasionally. Beat in the egg and vanilla until combined. Beat in as much of the flour as you can with the mixer. Stir in any remaining flour. If necessary, cover and chill dough until easy to handle.

**2** Shape dough into 1-inch balls. Place balls 2 inches apart on an ungreased cookie sheet. Bake in a 375°F oven for 7 minutes. Remove from oven; gently press a shallow indentation in each cookie with the back of a round ½-teaspoon measuring spoon. Return to oven and bake 2 minutes more or until bottoms are lightly browned. Transfer to a wire rack; cool.

**3** For filling, in a small saucepan combine chocolate pieces and sweetened condensed milk. Cook and stir over medium heat until chocolate is melted. Transfer to a pastry bag fitted with a small star tip. Pipe about 1 teaspoon of filling into the center of each cookie. Makes about 36 tartlets.

## Coconut-Cashew Pralines

*shown on page 81*

### WHAT YOU NEED

- 1½ **cups granulated sugar**
- 1½ **cups packed brown sugar**
- 1 **cup half-and-half or light cream**
- 3 **tablespoons butter**
- 2 **cups lightly salted roasted cashews**
- 1 **cup flaked coconut, toasted***

### HERE'S HOW

**1** Butter the sides of a 2-quart heavy saucepan about 7 inches in diameter.** In saucepan combine granulated sugar, brown sugar, and half-and-half. Cook and stir over medium-high heat until mixture boils. Clip a candy thermometer to side of pan. Reduce heat to medium-low; continue boiling at a moderate, steady rate, stirring occasionally, until the thermometer registers 234°F, soft-ball stage (16 to 18 minutes).

**2** Remove saucepan from heat. Add butter, but do not stir. Cool, without stirring, to 150°F (about 30 minutes).

**3** Remove thermometer from saucepan. Stir in cashews and coconut. Beat vigorously with a clean wooden spoon until mixture just begins to thicken but is still glossy (about 3 minutes).

**4** Working quickly, drop candy by spoonfuls onto waxed paper. Let stand until firm. Store tightly covered for up to 1 week. Makes about 60 candies.

*****Note:** To toast coconut, spread in a single layer in a shallow baking pan. Bake in a 350°F oven for 5 to 8 minutes or until light golden brown, watching carefully and stirring once or twice so the coconut doesn't burn.

******Note:** A saucepan with a smaller diameter will not allow for the necessary evaporation.

## Christmas Biscotti

*shown on page 82*

**WHAT YOU NEED** for the biscotti
**Vanilla Sugar**
- ⅓ **cup butter**
- 2 **teaspoons baking powder**
- ½ **teaspoon ground cardamom**
- 2 **eggs**
- 2 **cups all-purpose flour**
- ¾ **cup dried cranberries or snipped dried cherries**
- ¾ **cup chopped, shelled green pistachios**

**HERE'S HOW**

**1** To make Vanilla Sugar, fill a quart jar with 4 cups granulated sugar. Cut a vanilla bean in half lengthwise and insert both halves into the sugar. Secure lid and store in a cool dry place for several weeks before using. Will keep indefinitely.

**2** In a large mixing bowl beat the butter with an electric mixer on medium speed for 30 seconds. Add ⅔ cup of the Vanilla Sugar, baking powder, and cardamom; beat until combined. Beat in eggs. Beat in as much of the flour as you can with the mixer. Stir in any remaining flour and the cranberries and pistachios until combined. Divide dough in half. If necessary, cover and chill dough until easy to handle.

**3** Shape each portion of dough into a 9-inch roll. Place 4 inches apart on a lightly greased cookie sheet, flattening slightly to 2 inches wide.

**4** Bake in 375°F oven for 25 to 30 minutes or until a toothpick inserted near the center comes out clean. Cool rolls on the cookie sheet for 1 hour.

**5** Using a serrated knife, cut each roll diagonally into ¼-inch slices. Place slices, cut sides down, on an ungreased cookie sheet. Bake in a 325°F oven for 8 minutes. Turn slices over; bake 8 to 10 minutes more or until dry and crisp. Transfer to a wire rack to cool. Store in a tightly covered container at room temperature for up to 3 days or in the freezer for up to 3 months. Makes about 32 biscotti.

**WHAT YOU NEED** for the gift bag
- Printer paper; scissors
- Pencil
- 2 brown lunch sacks; cardboard
- Crafts knife; paintbrush; silver paint
- Thick white crafts glue; silver paper
- Metallic gold marker
- Star stickers
- Parchment paper

**HERE'S HOW**

**1** To make a tree pattern, fold the printer paper in half. Using the fold as the center, cut a tree shape smaller than the sack.

**2** Open pattern; place it on one sack front. Trace the right side of the pattern.

**3** Place cardboard in sack to protect back of sack. Use a crafts knife to cut along tree outline; fold back. Cut a whole tree shape from other sack. Paint one side silver; let dry. Fold in half. Glue fold to center of tree on sack. Cut silver paper to fit behind opening; glue in place. Let glue dry.

**4** Draw a 1×3-inch rectangle at the tree base; color gold. Cut three ¼×1-inch pieces from extra bag; glue on gold area as shown in photo, *page 82*. Let dry. Outline the tree shape using a gold marker. Add star stickers on the tree. Line bag with parchment paper.

## Braided Cranberry Bread with a Twist

*shown on page 83*

**WHAT YOU NEED**
- 2¾ **to 3 cups all-purpose flour**
- 1 **package active dry yeast**
- ½ **cup milk**
- ¼ **cup water**
- 2 **tablespoons granulated sugar**
- 2 **tablespoons butter or margarine**
- ½ **teaspoon salt**
- 1 **egg**
- ½ **cup finely chopped fresh cranberries**
- ¼ **cup packed brown sugar**
- 2 **tablespoons chopped pecans**
- 1½ **teaspoons finely shredded orange peel**
- ¼ **teaspoon ground cinnamon**
- ¼ **teaspoon ground nutmeg**
- ⅛ **teaspoon ground cloves**
- 1½ **teaspoons butter or margarine, melted**
  **Orange Icing**

**HERE'S HOW**

**1** In a large mixing bowl combine 1 cup of the flour and the yeast; set aside. In a medium saucepan heat and stir the milk, water, granulated sugar, the 2 tablespoons butter, and salt until warm (120°F to 130°F) and butter almost melts. Add milk mixture to flour mixture; add egg. Beat with an electric mixer on low to medium speed for 30 seconds, scraping sides of bowl constantly. Beat on high speed for 3 minutes. Use a wooden spoon to stir in as much of the remaining flour as you can.

**2** Turn dough out onto a floured surface. Knead in enough of the remaining flour to make a soft dough that is smooth and elastic (3 to 5 minutes total). Shape into a ball. Place in a lightly greased bowl; turn once. Cover and let rise in a warm place until double (1 to 1½ hours).

**3** Meanwhile, for filling, in a small bowl stir together cranberries, brown sugar, pecans, orange peel, cinnamon, nutmeg, and cloves; set aside.

**4** Punch down dough. Turn out onto lightly floured surface. Cover and let rest for 10 minutes. Grease a baking sheet. Roll dough into a 14×10-inch rectangle. Brush with the melted butter. Spread filling over dough. Starting from a long side, roll up dough. Seal seam. Cut roll in half lengthwise. Turn cut sides up. Loosely twist halves together, keeping the cut sides up. Pinch ends to seal. Place loaf on the prepared baking sheet. Cover; let rise in a warm place until nearly double (about 30 minutes).

**5** Bake in a 375°F oven about 25 minutes or until golden brown. Remove from baking sheet; cool on a wire rack. Drizzle with Orange Icing. Makes 1 loaf (18 servings).

**Orange Icing:** In a small bowl combine ½ cup sifted powdered sugar and enough orange juice (1 to 3 teaspoons) to make icing of drizzling consistency.

### Holiday Snowmen

*shown on page 84*

#### WHAT YOU NEED

- 1 18-ounce roll refrigerated chocolate chip, sugar, or peanut butter cookie dough
- 1 cup sifted powdered sugar
- ¼ teaspoon vanilla
- 1 to 2 tablespoons milk
  Gumdrops
  Miniature semisweet chocolate pieces

#### HERE'S HOW

**1** Cut cookie dough into 18 equal pieces. Divide each dough piece into 3 balls: one large (about 1¼ inches in diameter), one medium (about 1 inch in diameter), and one small (about ¾ inch in diameter). Assemble each set of balls ¼ inch apart in a snowman shape on an ungreased cookie sheet, placing the largest balls 2 inches apart so the snowmen don't bake together.

**2** Bake in a 375°F oven for 8 to 10 minutes or until edges are very lightly browned. Cool on cookie sheet for 3 minutes. Transfer cookies to a wire rack and let cool.

**3** For glaze, in a small bowl stir together powdered sugar, vanilla, and 1 tablespoon of the milk. Stir in additional milk, 1 teaspoon at a time, to make glaze of drizzling consistency. Spoon glaze over snowmen. Decorate as desired with gumdrops and/or chocolate pieces. Makes 18 cookies.

### Snickerdoodle Pinwheels

*shown on page 85*

#### WHAT YOU NEED

- ⅓ cup sugar
- 1 tablespoon ground cinnamon
- ½ cup butter, softened
- 1 3-ounce package cream cheese, softened
- 1 cup sugar
- ½ teaspoon baking powder
- 1 egg
- 1 teaspoon vanilla
- 2⅔ cups all-purpose flour
- 1 tablespoon butter, melted

#### HERE'S HOW

**1** For cinnamon-sugar mixture, in a small bowl combine the ⅓ cup sugar and the cinnamon; set aside.

**2** In a large mixing bowl beat the ½ cup butter and the cream cheese with an electric mixer on medium to high speed for 30 seconds. Add the 1 cup sugar and baking powder. Beat until combined, scraping sides of bowl occasionally. Beat in egg and vanilla until combined. Using the mixer, beat in as much of the flour as you can. Using a wooden spoon, stir in remaining flour.

**3** Divide dough in half. Roll half of dough between 2 sheets of waxed paper into a 12×8-inch rectangle. Remove top sheet of waxed paper. Brush dough with half of the melted butter. Sprinkle with 2 tablespoons of the cinnamon sugar.

**4** Starting from one of the short sides, roll up jelly-roll style, removing waxed paper as you roll. Seal edges. Repeat process with remaining dough, butter, and 2 tablespoons of cinnamon-sugar mixture. Roll each log in remaining cinnamon-sugar mixture. Wrap each log in plastic wrap or waxed paper. Chill about 4 hours or until firm.

**5** Using a sharp knife, cut logs into ¼-inch slices. Place slices 1 inch apart on an ungreased cookie sheet.

**6** Bake in a 375°F oven for 8 to 10 minutes or until edges are firm. Cool on cookie sheet for 1 minute. Transfer to a wire rack; cool. Makes 60 cookies.

# stockings were hung

*The old-world tradition of hanging stockings for Santa to fill is classier than ever.*

ST. NICK WILL CHUCKLE while filling Christmas socks as cleverly designed as these. **Damask Stocking,** *above*, stitches up quickly with few supplies. **Jolly Holiday Stockings,** *opposite*, are made from dish towels, felt, fleece, needlepoint canvas, and satin ribbon for a delightful mix of textures. Instructions and patterns are on pages 98–101.

*Choose neutral colors and*

The easy-to-make **Burlap Beauty**, *opposite*, features raw edges and topstitched patches for casual homespun style. As a homespun door ornament or to surprise your favorite gardeners,

*unusual materials to make spectacular stockings.*

the **Stuffed with Style** trio, *above*, is fun to shape from such novel materials as corrugated cardboard and leather lacing. Filled with gardening supplies, they are a welcome reminder that planting season will eventually return. Instructions are on page 102.

Designed to be filled with large and tiny treasures, **Pretty Pockets Stocking,** *above,* is a soft and textural beauty. For ride 'em cowboys, **Cowpoke Stocking,** *opposite,* has quilted Western-theme fabrics and a rough-and-tumble leather cuff accented with beads. Patterns and instructions are on pages 102–103.

Embellish kitchen linen to shape into charming **Mad for Plaid,**
*opposite*. Trimmed with jumbo rickrack and simple embroidery
stitches, this check stocking has a retro look for a bit of
holiday nostalgia. If you love to knit, gather needles and yarn
to make **Striped Stocking,** *above*, with red and green stripes
standing out on winter white. Instructions and patterns are on
pages 104–105.

## Damask Stocking

*shown on page 90*

### WHAT YOU NEED

Photocopier or tracing paper and
  pencil; scissors
1 yard red damask; 1½ yards of
  ¼-inch-diameter cording for
  piping or use purchased piping
Thread to match fabric and
  ribbons; straight pins
Sewing machine; needle
½ yard fusible fleece
¾ yard dark green fringe
4 to 6 yards 2-inch-wide red
  organdy ribbon
1¼ yards 1-inch-wide green
  velvet ribbon

### HERE'S HOW

**1** Enlarge and trace the pattern, *below;*
cut out.
**2** From damask cut two ½-yard pieces.
From one piece, cut and piece enough

**Damask Stocking**

2-inch-wide bias strips to cover cording
long enough to go all the way around the
stocking. Fold the bias strip over the
cording; stitch close to the cording.
**3** From remaining damask cut two
13×20-inch rectangles. Pin fleece to the
wrong side of each damask rectangle,
allowing 2 inches of damask to extend
beyond one short end for the top
hemmed edge of the stocking. Trim
excess fleece at the bottom edge. Fuse
the fleece to the damask.
**4** Layer the damask right sides facing.
Pin on the pattern, aligning the top

edge of the pattern with the fleece edge
at the top. Cut out the stocking front
and the back, adding ½-inch seam
allowances to the sides and foot.
**5** Fold under ½ inch on the top raw
edge of each stocking piece; fold under
again 1½ inches. Stitch close to fold.
**6** Align one end of the piping with the
top edge of the stocking front, matching
raw edges; pin. Stitch the piping to the
stocking front along the seam line. Trim
away excess piping.
**7** Right sides facing, pin the stocking
front to the stocking back along the seam
line; sew together. Clip the curves and
turn the stocking right side out.
**8** From damask cut a 3×6-inch strip.
Press under ½ inch on the long edges of
the strip; topstitch in place. Fold the
strip in half crosswise and tack to the
inside back of the stocking.
**9** For cuff, pin and sew fringe along the
top of the stocking. Cut off excess.
**10** To make a rose center, tightly wrap
organdy ribbon around a pencil
12 times; do not cut. Slide off the ribbon; hand-tack one end closed. To
make the petals, loosely twist the ribbon
tail into loops, bringing the ribbon back
to the tacked center at the end of each
loop. Tack each petal in place.
Continue making petals to complete
roses the shape and size you want. Tack
securely and trim the ends.
**11** To make the leaves, cut 4-inch lengths
from velvet ribbon. Right sides facing,
fold each length in half. Diagonally sew
from one corner of the top folded edge to
the center of the opposite edge. Trim
excess ribbon; turn leaves right side out.
Attach roses and leaves to stocking.

## Jolly Holiday Stockings

*shown on pages 90–91*

### FOR THE STRIPED DISH TOWEL
### STOCKING (A) YOU NEED

Photocopier or tracing paper and
  pencil; scissors; straight pins
2 red and white stripe linen dish
  towels; 24 inches of matching trim

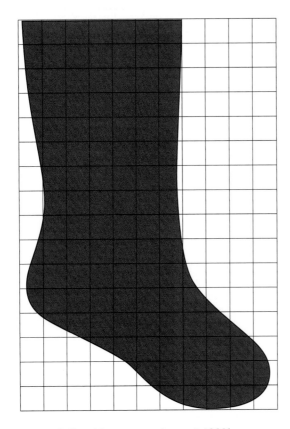

**Damask Stocking—reproduce at 400%**

1 square = 1 inch

Jolly Holiday Stockings

Thread; sewing machine; needle
Iron; 24 inches of jumbo red rickrack

**HERE'S HOW**

**1** Enlarge and trace the pattern, *below left*; add ½-inch seam allowances. Layer the towels; pin on the pattern aligning the towel hem with the upper edge of the stocking for the cuff. Cut out a stocking front and back.

**2** Right sides facing and leaving the top 8 inches of the stocking unstitched, sew the front to the back; trim. Zigzag-stitch seam allowances. Turn right side out.

**3** Sew the front to the back along the top 8 inches. Trim and zigzag-stitch the seam allowances. Fold over the cuff. Sew rickrack and trim to the cuff, using the photo, *above*, as a guide.

**4** Cut a 3×8-inch strip from dish towel fabric for a hanger. Fold the strip in half lengthwise, turn in raw edges, and press.

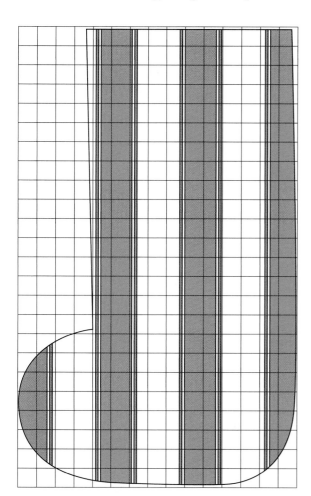

**A. Striped Dish Towel Stocking—reproduce at 500%**

1 square = 1 inch

**B. Cutout Tree Stocking—reproduce at 400%**

1 square = 1 inch

Topstitch ⅛ inch on both long edges. Cut raw ends at an angle. Fold under the raw edges. Sew the hanger to the back of the stocking cuff.

## FOR THE CUTOUT TREE STOCKING (B) YOU NEED

Photocopier or tracing paper and pencil; scissors
Small sharp embroidery scissors
½ yard *each* red and white felt
Thread; sewing machine; needle
Fade-away fabric marker
Pinking shears; fabric glue
7 small white pom-poms

### HERE'S HOW

**1** Enlarge the pattern, *page 99;* cut out. From white felt cut a rectangle 2 inches larger than the pattern. From red felt piece cut two rectangles 2 inches larger than the pattern.

**2** On the wrong side of one red felt, trace around the tree design; cut along the lines with embroidery scissors, removing the tree shape. Place tree cutout on the top, sandwich the white felt between the red felt pieces.

**3** Position the pattern on the layered felt. Lightly trace the pattern. Along the top sew ⅛ inch from the cut edges to hold one red and the white layer together. Sew all the layers together along the outline.

**4** With pinking shears cut the top (tree layer) of felt close to the stitched line. Cut the second (white) layer ¼ inch beyond the first and cut the third (red) layer ¼ inch from the white.

**5** For a hanger, from red felt cut a 1×8-inch strip; fold it in half and sew it to the inside back. Glue the pom-poms to the tree branches.

## FOR THE BEADED FRINGE STOCKING (C) YOU NEED

Photocopier or tracing paper and pencil; scissors; straight pins
1 yard white polar fleece; sewing machine; thread; needle; red bias tape; ¾ yard crystal beaded fringe with a decorative flange edge

### HERE'S HOW

**1** Enlarge the pattern, *below left,* adding ½-inch seam allowances. Add 8 inches to the top for the cuff. From fleece cut a stocking front and a back.

**2** Assemble the stocking the same as the Striped Dish Towel Stocking (A), *page 98.* For a hanger, cut 8-inch lengths of bias tape and beaded fringe. Snip the beads from the trim and sew the trim to the tape. Fold the hanger in half crosswise; sew it to the inside cuff.

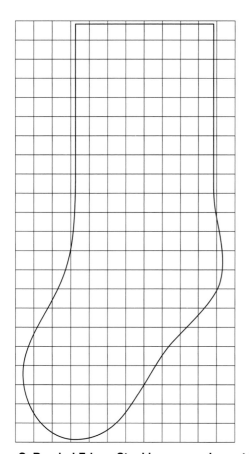

**C. Beaded Fringe Stocking—reproduce at 500%**

1 square = 1 inch

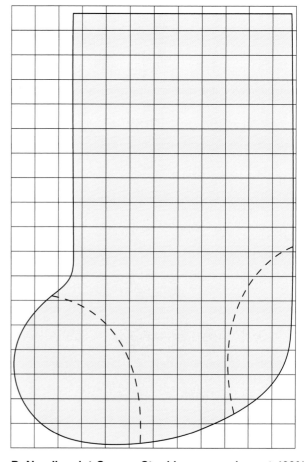

**D. Needlepoint Canvas Stocking—reproduce at 400%**

1 square = 1 inch

**3** Stitch beaded fringe to the center of the bias tape, then stitch the tape 1 inch from the cuff edge.

## FOR THE NEEDLEPOINT CANVAS STOCKING (D) YOU NEED
Photocopier or tracing paper and pencil; scissors
12×18-inches #10 white mono needlepoint canvas
Clip-art book of letters, stencils, or computer fonts; straight pins
12×18-inches red felt
3 to 4 strands of red wool tapestry yarn; tapestry needle
½-inch-wide red bias tape
Pencil or permanent marker

## HERE'S HOW
**1** Enlarge the stocking pattern, *opposite*, and trace onto canvas.

**2** If necessary, use a photocopier to enlarge letters to fit stocking. Lightly trace the letters onto the canvas. Stitch the letters and toe and heel outlines with wool yarn using cross stitches (see diagram, *below*).

 **Cross Stitch**

Cut out the stocking along the pattern lines.

**3** From felt cut a stocking back. For a hanger, from bias tape cut an 8-inch length; topstitch along the edges. Fold the tape in half crosswise; baste it to the wrong side of the felt back ½ inch from the outer corner. Sew bias tape to the top edges of stocking front and back, encasing raw edges.

**4** Wrong sides facing, pin the stocking front to the stocking back. Sew bias tape around the sides and foot, encasing raw edges and leaving the top edge open. Tack raw edges of the tape inside the stocking.

## FOR THE SATIN RIBBON STOCKING (E) YOU NEED
Photocopier or tracing paper and pencil; scissors
½ yard of white felt
Sewing machine
Red thread; needle
5 to 7 yards of 2-inch-wide double-faced red satin ribbon (more for fuller gathers, less for softer gathers)
8 inches of 1-inch-wide red satin ribbon for hanger

## HERE'S HOW
**1** Enlarge the pattern, *left*, adding ½-inch seam allowances. From felt cut out a stocking front and back.

**2** Sew a gathering stitch along one edge of the ribbon; pull up the gathers. Starting at the toe of the stocking front, topstitch the ribbon on the felt front. Trim the ends even with the felt. Sew another row of ribbon over the first, overlapping the ribbon to cover the gathering and stitching lines. Trim the ends even with the felt. Continue overlapping and sewing gathered ribbon to the stocking front, angling the ribbon slightly to accommodate curves.

**3** Right sides facing, sew the stocking front to the stocking back. Trim away excess ribbon from seam allowances. Turn the stocking right side out. Topstitch along the edges, leaving top open. For a hanger, fold the 1-inch-wide ribbon in half crosswise; sew it to the inside back of the stocking.

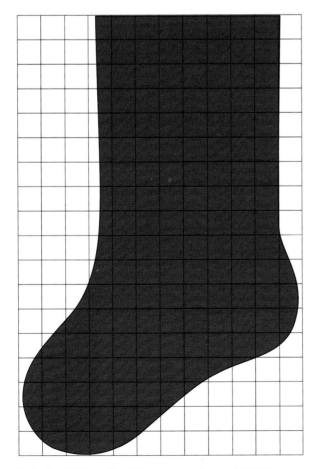

**E. Satin Ribbon Stocking—reproduce at 400%**

1 square = 1 inch

# clever wraps
# and containers

*Artistically wrap your holiday gifts using a
grand assortment of containers and supplies.*

"WOW" FRIENDS AND FAMILY with fresh wraps
that are gifts in themselves. Cover a woven basket in
natural texture for **Nutty Surprise,** *above*, and make a
coordinating card. **Pretty Pods,** *opposite*, are lovely
trims for a colorfully wrapped present and for later
hanging on a tree. Instructions are on page 116.

Simple painting and twisted-wire handles transform plain glass into Jolly Jars, *above*—just the right size for a puff of shredded paper and a candy cane or two. When the sweet treats are gone, place a tealight inside for a votive holder. Cookie Connoisseur, *opposite*, is quickly crafted using whatever ribbon and trims you have on hand, so you'll be prepared for gift giving at a moment's notice. Instructions are on pages 116–117.

*Pretty wraps can be made in little time and make lasting impressions.*

109

Give holiday cookies with style by crafting a Too-Cute Cookie Jar, *opposite*, that can be used long after your baked goods are gone. Purchased trims are a simple but festive solution for decorating the container. Bandanna Star Jar, *above*, holds a s'mores mix—but you could fill it with a variety of other delicious goodies. Instructions are on page 118.

Decorate a large clear glass container with snowflakes and mittens for Snow-Laden Treat Jar, *above*. Place colorful candy inside for crystal-clear contrast, and the look is complete. For beaders on your gift list, assemble the Jester-Style Jar, *opposite*, to hold oodles of shapes and sizes of beads. Instructions are on pages 118–119.

Give a blooming plant and fresh greenery in a Gilded Holiday Planter, *opposite*. The sparkly accents are scrapbook papers that add shapely color against a golden background. For a super simple presentation, put together See-Through Soap Jar, *above*, using a snippet of ribbon and a single ornament. Instructions are on page 119.

## Too-Cute Cookie Jar

*shown on page 110*

### WHAT YOU NEED

Star cookie cutter with knob
Pencil
Green felt
Pinking shears
Thick white crafts glue
Large jar with red lid
½-inch ribbon
Purchased garland
Scissors

### HERE'S HOW

**1** Trace around the star cookie cutter on green felt. Use pinking shears to cut out the star shape ¼ inch larger than the drawn lines.

**2** Glue the felt star to the lid. Glue the cookie cutter in the center of the felt. Tie a ribbon bow on the knob of the cookie cutter. Trim the ribbon ends.

**3** Glue the garland around the neck of the jar. Let the glue dry.

## Bandanna Star Jar

*shown on page 111*

### WHAT YOU NEED

Green bandanna
Scissors
Canning jar
Sewing machine and thread
S'mores mix, hot cocoa mix,
   or other treats
Silver star buckle
Fresh greenery

### HERE'S HOW

**1** From the green bandanna, cut a triangle large enough to fit around the neck of the jar. Hem the raw edge on a sewing machine.

**2** Fill the jar with hot cocoa mix or s'mores mix.

**3** Attach the bandanna to the jar by tying it through a silver star buckle. Tuck greenery under bandanna.

Snow-Laden Treat Jar

## Snow-Laden Treat Jar

*shown on page 112*

### WHAT YOU NEED

Thick white crafts glue
White wood snowflakes
Square jar with wire clamp closure
Beaded snowflake appliqués
Ribbon
Small knit ornaments
Scissors

### HERE'S HOW

**1** Glue the wood snowflakes on the jar and on the lid. Glue the appliqué snowflakes on the wood snowflakes. Let the glue dry.

**2** Use ribbon to tie ornaments to the wire clamp on the jar lid. Tie the ribbon ends into a bow; trim the ends.

Too-Cute Cookie Jar

Bandanna Star Jar

**Jester-Style Jar**

## Jester-Style Jar

*shown on page 113*

### WHAT YOU NEED

Medium-weight crafts wire in
   assorted colors
Scissors; ruler
Round pencil
Assorted beads; star and round
Jar with handle-style lid
Thick white crafts glue
Holiday trim

### HERE'S HOW

**1** Cut several 12-inch lengths of wire
and wrap around a pencil. Remove from
the pencil.

**2** Thread a bead on one end of each
wire, bending the wire ends to secure
the beads.

**3** Wrap the unbeaded wire ends around
the handle on the jar lid.

**4** Glue holiday trim around the neck of
the jar. Let the glue dry.

**5** Fill the jar with assorted colors,
shapes, and sizes of beads.

## Gilded Holiday Planter

*shown on page 114*

### WHAT YOU NEED

Metal container
Newspapers
Metallic gold spray paint
Adhesive-back metallic green
   vinyl paper, available in
   scrapbooking stores
Scissors
Gold glitter dimensional tube paint
Potted blooming plant
Fresh greenery

### HERE'S HOW

**1** Wash and dry the metal container.
In a well-ventilated work area, cover
the work surface with newspapers; place
the metal container on newspapers.
Lightly spray-paint two to three coats of
gold on the container, allowing each
coat to dry.

**2** Cut strips from adhesive-back
metallic paper. Remove protective
backing and apply the strips to the
painted container.

**3** Use the gold glitter tube paint to
outline the vinyl strips. Let the outline
paint dry.

**4** Insert a potted plant in the container;
fill in with fresh greenery.

**Gilded Holiday Planter**

**See-Through Soap Jar**

## See-Through Soap Jar

*shown on page 115*

### WHAT YOU NEED

Plastic candy trim
Strong glue for plastic and glass,
   such as E6000
Apothecary jar with lid
Craft wire
Holiday bath soaps
Small bath items
Ribbon

### HERE'S HOW

**1** Glue the candy decoration to the
knob of the jar lid using crafts wire to
secure. Let the glue dry.

**2** Fill the jar with holiday soaps and
small bath items.

**3** Tie a ribbon bow around the neck of
the jar.

# festive starters

*Enjoying good food with family and friends is a delightful holiday experience.*

SPECIAL DINNERS deserve impressive openers to set the stage for the food to follow. **Shrimp and Avocado Cocktail,** *opposite,* is a splendid first course. **Smoked Salmon Roll-Ups,** *above,* feature colorful tortillas to create an eye-catching hors d'oeuvre. Recipes are on page 128.

The essence of fresh herbs, garlic, wine, and orange makes **Herb-Baked Olives,** *above*, an incredibly delicious appetizer. You'll also enjoy the aroma that fills the kitchen during baking. **Ham and Cheese Stromboli Spirals,** *opposite,* are perfectly convenient party fare—beginning with a package of hot roll mix. For the dipping sauce, try the tangy flavors of **Dried Cherry Chutney.** Recipes are on page 129.

**Mushroom and Blue Cheese Tartlets,** *opposite*, are impressive appetizers that take little time to prepare, thanks to a base of purchased piecrust. Gorgonzola cheese is the pretty, golden topper. **Roasted Asparagus with Tomato Aïoli,** *above*, is finger food at its best. The aïoli is a simple flavored mayonnaise with spectacular taste. Recipes are on page 130.

It takes only three ingredients to make **Cheese 'n' Herb Mini Sweet Peppers,** *above*, hors d'oeuvres that will bring raves. Miniature sweet peppers serve as eye-catching vessels for the goat cheese filling. **Brie and Pears in Phyllo,** *opposite*, is a melt-in-your-mouth appetizer that will become a holiday mainstay. Sugared walnuts adorn the top of the golden package, while sautéed pears are nestled inside. Although it can be served with crackers, this elegant starter can also be served solo. Recipes are on page 131.

**Shrimp and Avocado Cocktail**

## Shrimp and Avocado Cocktail

*shown on page 120*

### WHAT YOU NEED

1½ **pounds fresh shrimp, frozen large shrimp in shells, or cooked, shelled, and deveined shrimp**
**Citrus-Horseradish Dressing**

2 **avocados, halved, pitted, peeled, and diced**

1 **medium orange, peeled, seeded, and sectioned, or ½ of an 11-ounce can mandarin orange sections, drained**

1 **tablespoon snipped fresh cilantro**

2 **teaspoons finely chopped, seeded fresh jalapeño chile pepper***
**Mixed torn salad greens, optional**
**Lime wedges, optional**

### HERE'S HOW

**1** Thaw shrimp, if frozen. Peel and devein shrimp. Cook shrimp in lightly salted boiling water for 1 to 3 minutes or until shrimp turn opaque, stirring occasionally. Rinse in a colander under cold running water; drain. Cover and chill for 2 hours or overnight.

**2** Prepare Citrus-Horseradish Dressing; set aside.

**3** For salad, in a medium bowl combine avocados, orange sections, cilantro, and jalapeño pepper. In a large bowl toss shrimp with the dressing.

**4** To serve, line 8 to 10 chilled glasses or serving-size plates with greens if desired. Top with avocado mixture. Arrange shrimp on avocado mixture. If desired, serve with lime wedges. Serve cocktails immediately. Makes 8 to 10 appetizer servings.

*Chile peppers contain oils that can burn your skin and eyes. Avoid direct contact with them by wearing plastic or rubber gloves. If your bare hands touch the peppers, wash your hands well with soap and water.

**Citrus-Horseradish Dressing:** In a screw-top jar, combine ¼ cup catsup, 2 tablespoons orange juice, 1 tablespoon salad oil, 2 teaspoons horseradish, ⅛ teaspoon salt, and ⅛ teaspoon cayenne pepper. Cover and shake well.

**Smoked Salmon Roll-Ups**

## Smoked Salmon Roll-Ups

*shown on page 121*

### WHAT YOU NEED

2 **cups cooked short grain or sticky rice, cooled**

2 **tablespoons sesame seeds, toasted**

2 **tablespoons rice vinegar**

2 **teaspoons sugar**

1 **teaspoon salt**

¼ **cup mayonnaise or salad dressing**

⅛ **teaspoon cayenne pepper**

4 **10-inch spinach- and/or tomato-flavored flour tortillas**

2 **3-ounce packages thinly sliced smoked salmon (lox-style)**

1 **medium avocado, halved, pitted, peeled, and sliced**

½ **medium cucumber, halved lengthwise, seeded, and cut into ½-inch sticks**

### HERE'S HOW

**1** In a medium bowl combine rice and sesame seeds. In a small bowl combine vinegar, sugar, and salt; stir to dissolve. Pour vinegar mixture over rice mixture; toss to coat. Set aside.

**2** Stir together mayonnaise and cayenne pepper; spread 1 tablespoon mayonnaise mixture over 1 tortilla. Spread ½ cup of the rice mixture on half of the tortilla; top with one-fourth of the salmon, avocado, and cucumber. Starting at the filled side, carefully and tightly roll up tortilla. Wrap in plastic wrap. Repeat with remaining tortillas, mayonnaise mixture, rice mixture, salmon, avocado, and cucumber. Chill at least 1 hour or up to 4 hours before serving.

**3** To serve, trim ends from rolls; discard. Cut rolls crosswise into 1-inch slices. If necessary secure with toothpicks. Makes 28 appetizers.

**Herb-Baked Olives**

**Ham and Cheese Stromboli Spirals**

## Herb-Baked Olives

*shown on page 122*

### WHAT YOU NEED

- 1¾ cups mixed imported Greek and/or Italian olives
- ½ cup dry white wine
- 5 tablespoons olive oil
- 2 4-inch sprigs fresh rosemary
- 1 tablespoon grated orange peel
- 2 tablespoons orange juice
- 1 tablespoon snipped fresh rosemary
- 1 tablespoon snipped fresh parsley
- 3 cloves garlic, minced
- ⅛ teaspoon black pepper

### HERE'S HOW

**1** In a 15×10×1-inch baking pan combine olives, wine, 2 tablespoons of the olive oil, and the rosemary sprigs, arranging olives in a single layer. Bake, uncovered, in a 375°F oven for 45 to 60 minutes or until most of the liquid has been absorbed, stirring occasionally.
**2** Meanwhile, for dressing, in a small bowl combine remaining 3 tablespoons olive oil, the orange peel, orange juice, rosemary, parsley, garlic, and pepper.
**3** Transfer cooled olive mixture to a medium bowl. Stir in the dressing. Cover and chill for at least 2 hours or up to 1 week. Makes seven ¼-cup servings.

## Ham and Cheese Stromboli Spirals

*shown on page 123*

### WHAT YOU NEED

- 1 16-ounce package hot roll mix
- ½ teaspoon dried basil, crushed
- 8 ounces cooked ham, chopped (2 cups)
- 1½ cups shredded baby Swiss or Gouda cheese (6 ounces)
- ⅔ cup dried cranberries
- 2 tablespoons butter or margarine, softened
- 1 egg
- 1 tablespoon water
  Dried Cherry Chutney, optional

### HERE'S HOW

**1** Line a 15×10×1-inch baking pan with foil; grease foil. Set aside. Prepare hot roll mix according to package directions, except stir the basil into the flour mixture. Knead as directed. Divide dough in half. Cover; let rest for 5 minutes.
**2** Meanwhile, for filling, in a medium bowl combine ham, Swiss cheese, and dried cranberries. Gently toss to mix.
**3** On a lightly floured surface roll each half of dough into a 10×8-inch rectangle. Spread 1 tablespoon of the softened butter on each dough rectangle, leaving a 1-inch border. Evenly sprinkle each rectangle with filling.
**4** Carefully fold edges of short sides over filling about 1 to 2 inches; roll up, beginning from a long side. Lightly moisten edges and ends with water and pinch to seal. Carefully place loaves,

seam side down, on the prepared baking pan. Cover; let rise in a warm place until nearly double in size (about 30 minutes). (Or cover loaves loosely with plastic wrap; chill overnight. Let stand at room temperature 20 minutes before baking.)
**5** In a small bowl combine egg and the water; brush over loaves. Bake in a 350°F oven for about 30 minutes or until golden brown. Cool on a wire rack for 30 minutes. Cut into ½-inch slices. If desired, serve with Dried Cherry Chutney for dipping. Makes 24 servings.

## Dried Cherry Chutney

*Serve with Ham and Cheese Stromboli Spirals*

### WHAT YOU NEED

- ½ cup dried tart red cherries
- ¼ cup water
- 2 tablespoons sugar
- 1 tablespoon finely chopped fresh ginger
- ¾ cup chutney

### HERE'S HOW

**1** In a small saucepan combine cherries, water, sugar, and ginger. Bring to boiling; cover and remove from heat. Let stand for 15 minutes.
**2** Snip any large pieces of chutney. Stir chutney into cherry mixture. Transfer to a serving bowl. Cover and chill for 2 to 24 hours. Makes 1⅓ cups.

Mushroom and Blue Cheese Tartlets

Roasted Asparagus with Tomato Aïoli

## Mushroom and Blue Cheese Tartlets

*shown on page 124*

### WHAT YOU NEED

- 2 **tablespoons butter**
- 2 **green onions, thinly sliced**
- 2 **cloves garlic, minced**
- 8 **ounces sliced baby portobello or button mushrooms**
- 2 **tablespoons dry sherry**
- 2 **tablespoons finely chopped walnuts, toasted**
- 1 **teaspoon snipped fresh thyme or ½ teaspoon dried thyme, crushed**
- ¼ **teaspoon black pepper**
- ½ **of a 15-ounce package folded refrigerated unbaked piecrust (1 crust)**
- ⅔ **cup crumbled Gorgonzola cheese or feta cheese (about 2½ ounces)**

### HERE'S HOW

**1** In a large skillet melt butter and cook green onions and garlic over medium heat for 1 minute. Add mushrooms and cook for 7 minutes. Remove skillet from heat. Add sherry to the skillet; return to heat. Cook and stir for 4 minutes. Stir in walnuts, thyme, and pepper. Remove from heat; let cool for 20 minutes.

**2** On a lightly floured surface unfold piecrust and roll to a 13-inch circle. Using a fluted 2¼-inch cookie cutter, cut 24 circles. Press circles into 1¾-inch muffin cups. Fill each tartlet with about 1 tablespoon of mushroom mixture. Top each tartlet with 1 teaspoon of cheese.

**3** Bake in a 375°F oven about 20 minutes or until edges of pastry are lightly browned. Cool for 5 minutes in pans. Remove from pans; serve warm. Makes 24 tartlets.

## Roasted Asparagus with Tomato Aïoli

*shown on page 125*

Aïoli (ay-OH-lee) is a French term for garlic-flavored mayonnaise.

### WHAT YOU NEED

- ¼ **cup mayonnaise or salad dressing**
- 3 **oil-packed sun-dried tomatoes, drained and snipped**
- 1 **teaspoon lemon juice**
- 1 **teaspoon snipped fresh basil or ½ teaspoon dried basil, crushed**
- 1 **clove garlic, minced**
- 1 **pound fresh asparagus spears**
- 2 **teaspoons olive oil or salad oil Seasoned salt, optional**

### HERE'S HOW

**1** For aïoli, in a small bowl stir together the mayonnaise, dried tomatoes, lemon juice, basil, and garlic.

**2** In a shallow roasting pan toss asparagus with oil. If desired, sprinkle lightly with seasoned salt. Spread asparagus in a single layer in the pan.

**3** Roast asparagus in a 450°F oven for 4 to 6 minutes or until crisp-tender. If desired, cut into 2-inch pieces. Serve with aïoli. Makes 4 servings.

**Note:** Rather than roasting, the asparagus dippers for this recipe can be steamed for 3 to 5 minutes, then chilled until serving time.

**Cheese 'n' Herb Mini Sweet Peppers**

## Cheese 'n' Herb Mini Sweet Peppers

*shown on page 126*

**WHAT YOU NEED**

- 30 red, yellow, and/or orange miniature sweet peppers (about 12 ounces total)
- 18 ounces semisoft goat cheese (chèvre)
- ¼ cup snipped fresh chives, tarragon, basil, or thyme Fresh chives or herbs, optional

**HERE'S HOW**

**1** Leaving the stem intact, cut a small opening along one side of each pepper. Remove the seeds; set peppers aside.
**2** In a small bowl combine goat cheese and snipped herb. Spoon cheese mixture evenly into prepared peppers. Arrange the filled peppers close together on a baking sheet.
**3** Bake filled peppers in a 350°F oven for 8 to 10 minutes or until cheese is heated through and peppers are crisp-tender. If desired garnish with fresh chives. Makes 30 peppers.

**Brie and Pears in Phyllo**

## Brie and Pears in Phyllo

*shown on page 127*

**WHAT YOU NEED**

- 1 15-ounce round Brie cheese
- 1 tablespoon butter
- 1 cup finely chopped pear
- 2 tablespoons orange marmalade
  Sugared Walnuts
- 8 sheets frozen phyllo dough (9×14-inch rectangles), thawed
- 3 tablespoons butter, melted Assorted crackers and/or bread

**HERE'S HOW**

**1** Slice Brie round in half horizontally, making two rounds; set aside.
**2** In a small saucepan heat 1 tablespoon butter until hot and cook the pear in the butter for 2 to 3 minutes or until pear is just tender; remove from heat and cool slightly. Spread orange marmalade over cut side of one of the Brie rounds. Top with half of the cooked pear and half of the Sugared Walnuts. Top with the remaining half of Brie, cut side down.
**3** Overlap two sheets of phyllo by 1 inch to create a 16×14-inch rectangle. Lightly brush with melted butter. Repeat with remaining phyllo.
**4** Place the Brie rounds in the center of the phyllo stack. Bring up phyllo sheets around Brie to enclose, pleating phyllo as necessary. Brush with the remaining butter. Bake in a 400°F oven for 12 to 15 minutes or until golden. Top Brie with remaining pear and Sugared Walnuts. Serve warm Brie immediately with crackers. Makes 20 servings.

**Sugared Walnuts:** In a small skillet combine ½ cup broken walnuts, 1 tablespoon sugar, and 1 tablespoon butter. Cook and stir over medium heat about 5 minutes or until walnuts are toasted. Pour mixture onto a piece of foil; let cool. Break into pieces if necessary.

# all through the house

*Sprinkle good tidings throughout your home with merry and bright handcrafted accents.*

YOUR HOME WILL SHINE with symbols of the glorious season. **Eucalyptus Topiaries,** *above,* in traditional red and green, contribute color and texture to a tabletop or mantel. **St. Nick Pillow and Stocking,** *opposite,* are tributes to everyone's favorite elf. Instructions start on pages 140–141.

Wrap your table in red and white with **Snowflakes on Parade,** *above*. Buttons accent snowflake cutouts, and contrasting blanket stitches trim the edge. For a framed sensation, use colorful papers to cut and layer **Oh-So-Happy Santa,** *opposite*. He'll spread the joy of the season in the wink of an eye. Patterns and instructions are on pages 141–142.

White and gold are an exquisite combination in **Wonderfully Woven Runner,** *opposite*. Crafted from white wool felt and half a dozen different ribbons, the runner will be admired for its star-studded design. **So Charmed,** *above*, will make your holiday table sparkle with style and color. Patterns and instructions are on pages 142–143.

Greet carolers and guests with a **Delightful Door Trim,** *above*.
Prestitched letters make this project a breeze to assemble or to
personalize with your family's name. **Star Parade,** *opposite,* are
a playful addition to mantel displays. The painted designs are
so simply stated that kids will be eager to make a galaxy of
their own. Instructions are on pages 144–145.

## Delightful Door Trim

*shown on page 138*

### WHAT YOU NEED

Scissors; mat board
3 silver frames with 2×3-inch
　openings
Fleece
5×12-inch piece of green silk fabric
Fabric glue
1½-inch appliqué letters
Three 1-inch poinsettia appliques
1-inch cabone ring
Red pearl cotton
2 yards of 3-inch-wide red
　satin ribbon
Evergreens
Jingle bell

### HERE'S HOW

**1** Cut a piece of mat board to fit each frame; cover with fleece and silk fabric;

Star Parade

glue in place. Glue a letter and poinsettia in the center of each frame.
**2** Single-crochet around the cabone ring with pearl cotton.
**3** Determine the length of the ribbon banner. Slip the ribbon over the cabone ring and fuse or stitch the layers together.
**4** Glue the frames to the ribbon.
**5** Use ribbon to tie a bow, evergreens, and a jingle bell to the top of the door decoration.

## Star Parade

*shown on page 139*

### WHAT YOU NEED

Tracing paper
Pencil
1-inch-thick insulation foam panel
Hand saw with fine blade
Wood file
Paintbrush
Acrylic paints in red, yellow, black,
　green, and lime green
$\frac{5}{16}$-inch wood dowels
Drill press of hand drill with
　$\frac{5}{16}$-inch drill bit
2-inch-square wood blocks
Wood sealer, such as First Step

Awl
Adhesive for foam, such as Hold
　the Foam
Wood glue
Craft wire in green, yellow, and red

### HERE'S HOW

**1** Trace or photocopy the star patterns, *opposite*. Cut out. Trace the patterns onto insulation foam. Cut out stars using a saw. Smooth the rough edges with a wood file.
**2** Paint stars with two coats of assorted color acrylic paints. Let dry.
**3** Cut wood dowels in various heights. Drill holes in the center of wood blocks to insert dowels. Apply wood sealer to dowels and wood blocks. Let dry. Paint dowels black and blocks assorted colors.
**4** Insert dowel rods in stars by starting a hole in the foam with an awl. Use foam glue to secure the foam to the dowel. Glue dowels in blocks using wood glue.
**5** From the base of the wood dowel for each star, wrap colored wire on the dowel. Decorate each star with wire, as shown in the photo, *above*.

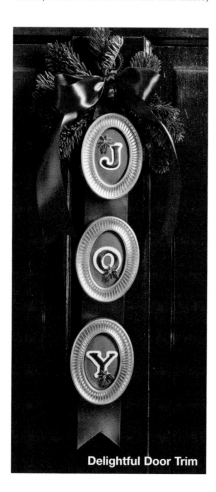

Delightful Door Trim

Star Parade Patterns—
reproduce at 200%

# holiday ways with paper

*Weave an assortment of beautiful scrapbook papers into holiday creations.*

CHOOSING PAPERS IS SO MUCH FUN, especially when you have a craft in mind. **Symbolic Greetings,** *opposite*, use check papers to back chenille-stem designs, and **Holiday Lights,** *above*, spins the center light motif from the background paper. Instructions are on page 156.

Use scrapbooking techniques to craft **Believe**, *above*, for a special friend. Start with a snowman sticker, and the rest is just as easy. To make **Fill-Your-Heart Cards,** *opposite,* coordinating papers are key. Select three to match holiday stickers. With a few cuts and strategic placement, you'll have festive, professional-looking cards. Instructions start on page 157.

JOY

May your Christmas dreams...

...be filled with magic!

Let it fill your HEART this Christmas

May peace be more than

Layered papers are torn and lifted from the backgrounds on the glittered **Holly-Filled Hellos**, *opposite*. Folded shapes, contemporary and traditional, are decorated with gold cutouts and paint for glittering **Starred Salutations**, *above*. Instructions and patterns are on pages 158–159.

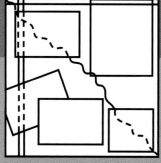

Capture the unwrapping of a special gift. **A Kitty for Christmas** scrapbook page, *below*, is a lovely example of organizing special memories.

December 25, 2001 | Bailey Age 8
For months, Bailey had been asking for a kitty with no success. Finally, she decided to ask Santa via his website to bring her a kitty for Christmas. We never expected him to actually come through, but on Christmas morning, Bailey peeked over the balcony and saw something suspicious under the tree. Could it really be? No, it's not possible....Wait! It's a kitty! A brown and black striped 11-month old kitten with a red collar! Bailey named her Tinsel, since she arrived on Christmas morning. She could not have been more excited!

Add sparkle with narrow metallic ribbon.

Diagonally tear a 12-inch piece of pattern paper to accent the background.

Chalk paper edges to create vintage appeal.

Mount some of the letters on adhesive spacers to lift them from the page.

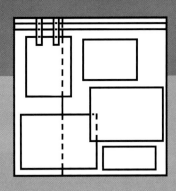

For a school concert or holiday performance, **Children's Christmas Musical**, *below*, shows easy techniques for scrapbooking the season's memories.

Place program on a wide strip of patterned paper.

Overlap bands of color to create a plaid design.

Photocopy a program in reduced size to fit on the page.

Use eyelets for page accents.

Fabric stickers carry out the holiday theme.

153

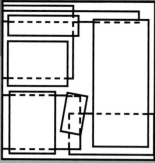

Recall nights waiting for St. Nick's appearance with photos, a child's letter to Santa, and special memorabilia as on this **Tonight the World is a Sweeter Place** page.

Layer photos on solid and check papers.

Create the headline using a script with shadow font.

Stamp, chalk, and tear paper edges to add texture and interest.

Attach for safekeeping a child's letter to Santa Claus.

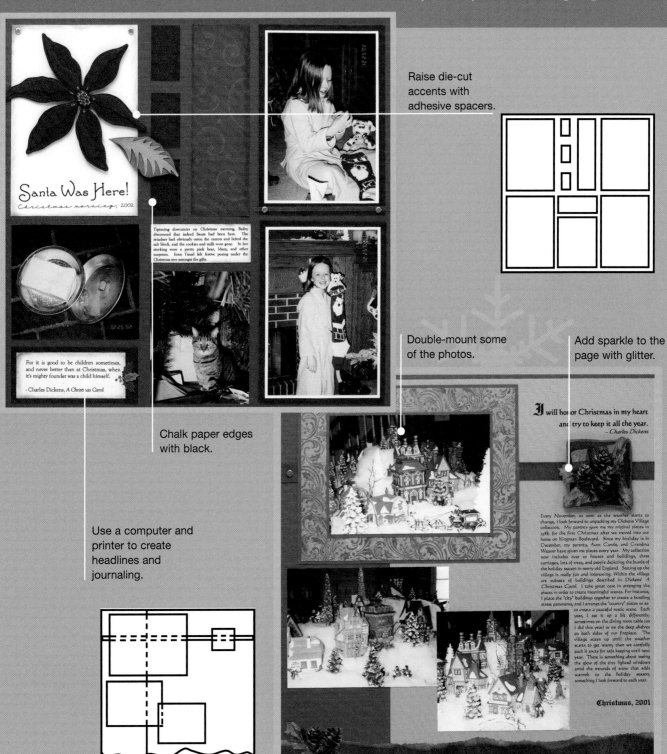

Raise die-cut accents with adhesive spacers.

Double-mount some of the photos.

Add sparkle to the page with glitter.

Chalk paper edges with black.

Use a computer and printer to create headlines and journaling.

Choose traditional red and green to set the stage for Christmas scrapbook pages. **Santa Was Here** and **Let Us Honor Christmas** share wonderful techniques and layout options to make your album shine with holiday spirit.

## Symbolic Greetings

*shown on page 146*

**WHAT YOU NEED**

Scrapbook paper in black, gold dot, and black/gray check for the star card; ruler
Scissors; hot-glue gun; glue sticks
Chenille stems in metallic gold, metallic green, metallic red, and green
Crafts knife; metallic silver paint pen
24-gauge gold wire; wire snips
Tape; double-sided tape
Scrapbook paper in red check and black for the tree card
Green chenille stems

**HERE'S HOW**

**1** *For the star card,* fold an 8½×11-inch rectangle of black paper in half. Cut a 4½×7-inch rectangle of gold dot paper. Cut a 4×6½-inch rectangle of black/gray check paper.

**2** Shape one piece of metallic gold chenille stem into a star. Twist ends together to secure.

**3** Lay the star on black/gray check paper. Trace inside the star shape onto paper. Using a crafts knife, cut out the star. Draw small lines around the star

**Symbolic Greetings**

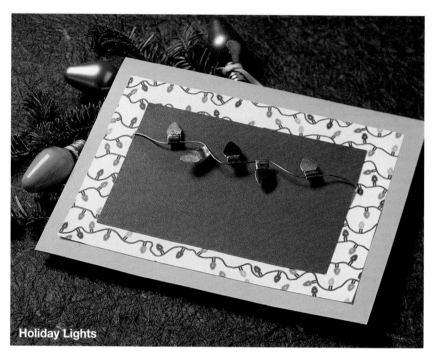
**Holiday Lights**

using a silver paint pen. Lay metallic star on check paper. Using a crafts knife, cut a small slit under the star on each side. Use 3 inches of gold wire to wrap over the metallic star and thread through the check paper. Twist wires to secure and tape them to the back of the check paper. Using double-sided tape, adhere the gold paper to the black card. Adhere the black/gray check to the gold paper. Hot-glue the star in place.

**4** *For the tree card,* fold a 8½×11-inch sheet of red check paper in half. Cut a 3×6-inch piece of black paper and adhere it to the front of the red card using double-sided tape.

**5** Shape a green non-metallic chenille stem into a long triangle. Diagonally wrap a green metallic chenille stem across the triangle.

**6** Cut a gold metallic chenille stem in half. Coil one section and attach it to the top of the triangle. Cut the remaining half into three short pieces; tuck into coiled piece. Fold a red metallic chenille stem into a stacked zigzag shape; attach to the bottom of the tree as the trunk. Hot-glue the tree in place.

**Holiday Lights Patterns**

## Holiday Lights

*shown on page 147*

**WHAT YOU NEED**

Scrapbook paper in lime green and fuchsia; scissors
String of lights scrapbook paper
Green 22-gauge crafting wire
Wire snips
Masking tape
Carbon paper; pencil
Emboss metal, such as ArtEmboss, in bright red, bright gold, cerulean blue, and mint green
Double-sided tape

**HERE'S HOW**

**1** Fold the green paper in half and trim to card size. Cut the string of lights paper to coordinate with the card size. Cut the fuchsia paper smaller.

**2** Cut green wire approximately 10 inches long. Bend curves in the wire and attach it to the back of the fuchsia paper with masking tape.

**Believe**

## Fill-Your-Heart Cards

*shown on page 149*

### WHAT YOU NEED for the joy card

  Card stock in dark red, beige,
    and dark green
  Scissors
  Glue stick
  Snowmen sticker and small
    coordinating sticker
  Brown chalk
  Joy stamp
  Black ink pad
  Coordinating print paper
  Computer and printer

### HERE'S HOW

**1** Fold the dark red card stock in half and trim to card size.
**2** Cut beige paper slightly smaller than the card front. Cut a rectangle from green card stock, trimming slightly smaller than the beige paper. Glue the rectangles to the card front.
**3** Apply a sticker to beige card stock, trim, and chalk the edges.
**4** Stamp JOY vertically on beige card stock, trim, and chalk the edges. Mount the stamped paper on dark red and trim a narrow border.

**3** Trace and cut out the lightbulbs and socket patterns, *opposite*. Using carbon paper, trace the bulb onto red, gold, and blue metal and the socket onto green metal. Cut out the shapes.
**4** Using double-sided tape, secure the back of a light socket to the front of a metal light. Wrap it around the wire to secure.
**5** Layer and adhere the string of lights paper and fuchsia paper to the card using double-sided tape.

## Believe

*shown on page 148*

### WHAT YOU NEED

  Card stock in light blue, white,
    and dark blue; scissors
  Snowman sticker
  Chalk; computer and printer
  Glue stick; silver brads
  Adhesive spacers, such as
    Pop Dots

### HERE'S HOW

**1** Fold the light blue card stock in half and trim to card size.
**2** Tear white card stock large enough to accommodate the sticker. Chalk the edges. Adhere the sticker in the center.

**3** Print "believe" on white card stock and trim in a strip to fit the width of the card. Glue on dark blue card stock; trim narrow borders. Use brads to attach the strip to the card front.
**4** Use adhesive spacers to attach the stickered paper above the strip.

Fill-Your-Heart Cards

**5** Cut a strip from print paper. Glue across the card front. Glue the stickered and stamped papers on the strip.

**6** For the inside, glue a print strip across the center. Print "Let it fill your HEART this Christmas" on beige card stock. Tear and chalk the edges. Place a small sticker on beige paper, trim, and chalk the edges. Glue the sticker and message on the print strip.

**WHAT YOU NEED for the dreams card**

- Card template, such as Deluxe Cuts
- Pencil
- Card stock in dark green, beige, and light green
- Scissors
- Chalk
- Coordinating print paper
- Holiday stickers
- Computer and printer
- Glue stick
- Brads
- Crafts knife

**HERE'S HOW**

**1** Trace the template on card stock; cut out. Chalk the edges of the papers. Place stickers on some of the paper pieces.

**2** Print "May your Christmas dreams…" and "…be filled with magic!" on beige card stock. Trim and chalk the edges.

**3** Adhere the paper pieces to the card front, attaching the message with a brad.

**4** For the inside, cut two small squares from light green and the print papers. Arrange the squares and a sticker on the inside of the card. Glue the decorative elements in place.

Holly-Filled Hellos

## Holly-Filled Hellos

*shown on page 150*

**WHAT YOU NEED for the accordion card**

- Scissors
- Red, cream, and green card stock
- Ruler; holly stickers; print paper
- Computer and printer
- Adhesive spacers, such as Pop Dots; glue stick
- Metallic gold glitter pen

**HERE'S HOW**

**1** Cut the red card stock 3×12 inches. Accordion-fold the paper every 3 inches.

**2** Adhere a sticker to print paper; trim. Mount the paper on contrasting card stock and trim.

**3** Print messages on cream card stock to fit card size. Tear around each message.

**4** Use adhesive spacers to attach the sticker card stock to the card front. Glue the messages in the card.

**5** Use a glitter pen to enhance the sticker. Let dry.

**WHAT YOU NEED for the peace card**

- Card stock in dark green, red, and cream; scissors; holly sticker
- Computer and printer
- Chalk; glue stick
- Adhesive spacers, such as Pop Dots; metallic gold glitter pen

**HERE'S HOW**

**1** Fold green card stock in half; trim to the card size.

**2** Double-mat the sticker; trim.

**3** Print "May peace be more than a season…" on cream card stock and tear the top edge. Chalk the edges.

**4** Cut a strip from red card stock for the card front. Tear along the bottom.

**5** Glue the paper pieces on the card front, using adhesive spacers to mount the stickered paper. Print a desired message for the inside of the card on cream and tear it in a strip. Glue the message inside the card.

**6** Use a glitter pen to enhance the sticker. Let dry.

## Starred Salutations

*shown on page 151*

### WHAT YOU NEED

Tracing paper; pencil
Scissors
Two-tone green striped scrapbook
    paper (for tree) and two-tone red
    stripe paper (for star)
Muted gold scrapbook paper
Carbon paper
Iridescent gold dimensional paint,
    such as Scribbles
Hole punch
Double-sided tape; paper stars

### HERE'S HOW

**1** *For the tree card,* enlarge and trace the pattern, *below right,* and cut out the tree shape. Fold the green striped paper in half; trace around the pattern, making the left edge the hinge. Trace around star pattern on gold paper; cut out shapes.
**2** Place carbon paper between the card front and the pattern; trace the tree branches and trunk. Trace lines using dimensional paint. Let the paint dry.
**3** Punch circles from gold paper. Using double-sided tape, adhere star and circles to the tree.
**4** *For the star card,* enlarge and trace the pattern, *right,* and cut out. Fold the red strip paper in half and trace around the pattern, making a hinge at the left star point. Cut out the stars.
**5** Draw wavy lines on each star point using dimensional paint. Let dry for several hours.
**6** Using double-sided tape, adhere three gold stars to the center front of the card.

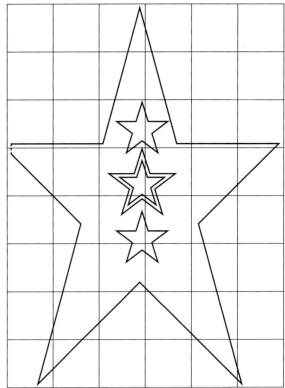

**reproduce at 200%**   1 square = 1 inch

**Starred Salutations**

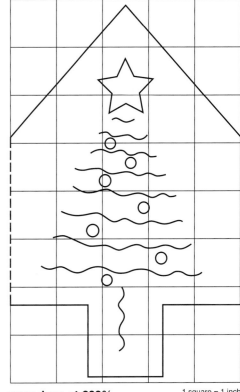

**reproduce at 200%**   1 square = 1 inch

# index

# sources

**APPLIQUÉS**
Hirschberg Schutz & Co., Inc.
Union, NJ 07083

Joy Insignia, Inc.
Deerfield Beach, FL  33443

Wrights
P.O. Box 398
West Warren, MA 01092
www.wrights.com

**BRADS**
Magic Scraps
magicscraps.com

**CARD STOCK**
Bazzill Basics Paper
bazzillbasics.com

**FIBERS**
Cut-It-Up
530/389-2233
cut-it-up.com

**TRIMS**
Provo Crafts & Novelty Inc.
Spanish Fork, UT 84660

Westrim Crafts
www.westrimcrafts.com

**YARN**
Adriafil
www.adriafil.com